Affinity Online

CONNECTED YOUTH AND DIGITAL FUTURES
Series Editor: Julian Sefton-Green

This series explores young people's day-to-day lives and futures. The volumes consider changes at the intersection of civil and political reform, transformations in employment and education, and the growing presence of digital technologies in all aspects of social, cultural, and political life. The John D. and Catherine T. MacArthur Foundation's Digital Media and Learning (DML) Initiative has supported two research networks that have helped launch this series: the Youth and Participatory Politics Research Network and the Connected Learning Research Network. The DML Initiative and the DML Hub at the University of California, Irvine also support production and open access for this series.

connectedyouth.nyupress.org

By Any Media Necessary: The New Activism of American Youth
Henry Jenkins, Sangita Shresthova, Liana Gamber-Thompson,
Neta Kligler-Vilenchik, and Arely Zimmerman

The Class: Living and Learning in the Digital Age
Sonia Livingstone and Julian Sefton-Green

*The Digital Edge: How Black and Latino Youth Navigate
Digital Inequality*
S. Craig Watkins, Alexander Cho, Andres Lombana-Bermudez,
Vivian Shaw, Jacqueline Vickery, and Lauren Weinzimmer

Affinity Online: How Connection and Shared Interest Fuel Learning
Mizuko Ito, Crystle Martin, Rachel Cody Pfister, Matthew H. Rafalow,
Katie Salen, and Amanda Wortman

Affinity Online

How Connection and
Shared Interest Fuel Learning

Mizuko Ito

Crystle Martin

Rachel Cody Pfister

Matthew H. Rafalow

Katie Salen

Amanda Wortman

NEW YORK UNIVERSITY PRESS
New York

NEW YORK UNIVERSITY PRESS
New York
www.nyupress.org

References to Internet websites (URLs) were accurate at the time of writing. Neither the author nor New York University Press is responsible for URLs that may have expired or changed since the manuscript was prepared.

Library of Congress Cataloging-in-Publication Data

Names: Ito, Mizuko, editor.
Title: Affinity online : how connection and shared interest fuel learning / edited by
    Mizuko Ito, Crystle Martin, Rachel Cody Pfister, Matthew H. Rafalow, Katie Salen,
    and Amanda Wortman.
Description: New York : New York University Press, [2019] | Includes bibliographical
    references and index.
Identifiers: LCCN 2018021512 | ISBN 9781479801923 (cl : alk. paper) |
    ISBN 9781479852758 (pb : alk. paper)
Subjects: LCSH: Online social networks—Case studies. | Youth—Social networks—Case
    studies. | Education—Effect of technological innovations on—Case studies. | Internet
    in education—Case studies.
Classification: LCC HM742 .A42 2018 | DDC 302.30285—dc23
LC record available at https://lccn.loc.gov/2018021512

New York University Press books are printed on acid-free paper, and their binding materials are chosen for strength and durability. We strive to use environmentally responsible suppliers and materials to the greatest extent possible in publishing our books.

Manufactured in the United States of America

10 9 8 7 6 5 4 3 2 1

Also available as an ebook

Contents

Note on the Text

This book is a synthesis of two years of collaborative ethnographic field-work conducted by members of the Leveling Up project, part of the MacArthur Foundation–funded Connected Learning Research Network and headed by Mizuko Ito and Katie Salen at the University of California, Irvine. Members of the Leveling Up research team include Adam Ingram-Goble of MINDBODY, Inc., Ksenia Korobkova of UC Irvine, Yong Ming Kow of City University of Hong Kong, Crystle Martin of El Camino College, Rachel Cody Pfister of UC San Diego, Matthew H. Rafa-low of YouTube, Amanda Wortman of UC Irvine, and Timothy Young of Twitch. Members of the Media, Activism, and Participatory Politics (MAPP) project led by Henry Jenkins at the University of Southern California (USC), and part of the Youth and Participatory Politics Research Network (YPP), have also contributed case material. Neta Kligler-Vilenchik of Hebrew University of Jerusalem and Sangita Shresthova of USC represent the MAPP researchers contributing case material.

This book is the result of a collaborative process of joint analysis and writing that built on our earlier experiences in the Digital Youth Project (Ito et al. 2010). Research protocols and codes were coordinated across the diverse case studies, and the insights and themes in this book grew out of iterative shared analysis. Unlike a traditional edited volume in which case studies are broken out chapter by chapter, in this book each chapter includes examples from multiple cases. In other words, it is a co-authored volume to which all authors contributed throughout the book. Each chapter has one or more lead authors who took responsibility for the writing, but every chapter incorporates material and input from a wide range of co-authors and the case studies they represent. Individual researchers who led on specific case studies have written brief case overviews and learner stories that are broken out from the main text. The full range of people who have contributed to this project and this book are mentioned in the acknowledgments. The case studies interspersed through the book are presented in a more traditional single-author format, written by the authors who led on the fieldwork for the case.

The case studies and approaches that the co-authors brought to the writing have been diverse, but we have agreed on certain conventions to provide some consistency:

- Chapter 1 provides background on how the project was organized and an overview of the cases. More detailed case reports on the five individual research studies conducted by members of the Leveling Up team between the years 2011 and 2013 are provided online at http://clalliance.org/publications/.
- The case studies were conducted using different data collection methodologies, and we have varying degrees of contextual information about our participants. In every case, if we know the information, then we have indicated age, gender, location, and what each participant self-identified as his or her racial or ethnic identity. If this information is not indicated, it means that we did not know the information for this participant because of the constraints of the particular case study. For example, in some of the studies that focus on online affinity networks, interviews were conducted over the phone or through online chat. In most cases, we derived this information from self-reports in background questionnaires we administered after most of our formal interviews. Although race is not always an analytic category relevant to our description, we thought that if racial or ethnic identity were to be mentioned for some number of participants, then we needed to be consistent in our treatment and indicate racial identity for all respondents for whom we did have this information.
- In referring to the online affinity networks studied, we have chosen to use the real names of the communities, except in instances in which the communities were relatively small and identifying the community would increase the likelihood of participants being identified, such as in the cases of the *Wrestling Boards* and *Sackboy Planet*.
- We have used pseudonyms in most cases when referring to our research participants. In some cases, our participants chose these pseudonyms. For adult participants, we offered the option of using their screen names or their real-life names. We believe that giving participants this choice allows for public recognition and honors the positive reputations that they have developed through their online affinity networks. When real names or screen names are used, we indicate this by notes to the text.

1

Introduction

Amy was 17 years old when she was interviewed as part of Pfister's (2014, 2016) study of Ravelry.com, an online community for knitters and crocheters. Amy is an avid fiber crafter and pattern maker, and she is also active on *Hogwarts at Ravelry*, a group within Ravelry focused on *Harry Potter*–related creations (the case study appears at the end of chapter 4). Amy first learned to crochet from her grandmother and picked up knitting with her sister. Eventually she started to look online for designs and inspiration, and one of her friends introduced her to Ravelry. There she found a wealth of resources, new designs, and kindred spirits, including the subcommunity of *Harry Potter* fans. One of Amy's hat designs, inspired by a hat in the sixth *Harry Potter* movie, has been "favorited" by 1,100 people and is in the queue of more than 400 people as something that they would like to make. She has begun selling her patterns on Ravelry and, with the support of her father, is planning to launch a blog and expand her business online. Her passion for the fiber arts has even sparked a similar interest in her parents. Her mother has started to crochet, and her father has picked up knitting.

Although Amy's story has much that is familiar to earlier generations, it is worth noting some important differences. In an earlier era, Amy would have pursued her interest in knitting and crocheting with her family, friends, and possibly eventually a local knitting circle or related group. She may have been able to find others in her Colorado community who could have introduced her to the intricacies of pattern design, but it is unlikely that she would have found a critical mass of knitters who are also *Harry Potter* fans. While she might have designed a *Harry Potter*–inspired hat based on her personal interest, she would not have connected with thousands of other *Harry Potter* fans who also appreciated her design. It is also unlikely that she would have been able to sell and market her designs, given the niche nature of the audience and the lack of distribution channels in local communities. The online affinity network of Ravelry, and opportunities for online distribution and sales, vastly expanded Amy's ability to pursue a specialized interest, develop expertise, and connect this interest to future opportunities.

Young people such as Amy are growing up in an environment of abundant connection to information, knowledge, and social interaction that offers new opportunities for learning and pursuing interests. Activities such as quickly googling for information, posting questions on specialized online forums, or publishing creative work online are now commonplace. It is easy to forget that it has been less than a decade since these kinds of interactions became widespread in the United States. And while these practices have been spreading with breathtaking speed through the everyday social exchanges of teens, our schools, policies, community institutions, and workplaces have been slower to respond. Many young people are taking to digital tools and networks to connect with communities of interest, gain specialized skills and expertise, and engage in shared projects and causes, but in our research we found relatively few instances of young people connecting these activities to economic opportunities or school. Examples such as Amy's, in which parents are actively supporting the connection between online interests and other opportunities, were relatively rare. The majority of young people we spoke to did not find ways of connecting the learning in their online affinity networks with in-school, civic, or career-relevant opportunities.

These findings are consistent with findings from our prior fieldwork in 2006–2007 for the Digital Youth Project, which cast a wide net in documenting young people's new media practices during the first large wave of social media adoption in the United States. We documented how gaming and social media were becoming primary vehicles for social hanging out, and we also found many examples of young people mobilizing online tools and networks to "geek out" with others online and go deep into areas of interest. While we recognized how these settings were enabling new and powerful forms of interest-driven, informal, and social learning, we also noted how relatively few young people were taking full advantage of the learning potential of digital networks. Even fewer were going on to connect their informal learning to future opportunity in academic, civic, and career-relevant settings. This disconnect between the tremendous opportunity for learning that the online world offers and the relatively low uptake, particularly among less resourced and less tech-savvy young people, is cause for concern (Ito et al. 2013).

Building on the Digital Youth Project, the Leveling Up study was designed to focus on online practices and networks that could bridge the divides between in-school and out-of-school learning. For our case studies, we sought out online communities that are both highly engaging to youth and also tied to academic, career, and civic practices. We also tried to include interest areas that attracted youth historically underrepresented in technology-related areas, specifically girls and youth with lower socioeconomic status. Our case studies include tech-savvy groups of gamers as well as less stereotypically "geeky" communities, such as knitters and fans of boybands and professional wrestlers. Through these cases, we investigated the supports that connect young people's interests to opportunity—such as Amy's father supporting her emerging online business—as well as missed opportunities and disconnects that inhibit this kind of connection and brokering.

To understand the implications of these points of connection and disconnection, we draw from the model of connected learning. Connected learning is a "synthetic model of learning" (Penuel et al. 2016); it both describes a form of meaningful and opportunity-enhancing learning and guides design and policies that expand access to this form of learning. The model grows out of an expanding body of evidence that learning is resilient and meaningful when it is tied to social relationships and cultural identities, and when it spans in-school and out-of-school settings. As a model for design and social change, connected learning focuses on connecting young people's interests and peer culture to opportunity and recognition in academic, civic, and career-relevant settings. Connected learning strives for equity by embracing the cultural identities of diverse young people, meeting them where they are in their communities of interest, and building points of connection and translation to opportunity in schools, employment, and civic and political institutions.

Connected learning differs from more traditional learning and reform approaches in that it is centered on young people's interest-driven learning and is agnostic as to the types of relationships and institutions that can support this learning. While teachers and classrooms are critical in the learning of most young people, we also see online communities and communication, and caring adults at home and in their local communities, as valuable supports for learning. By focusing on shared interests and social practices, connected learning draws attention to how social relationships and networks fuel learning and broker opportunities in varied settings, including online affinity networks.

The Leveling Up study was designed to investigate the role that online affinity networks play, and could potentially play, in connected learning. We are still far from realizing a world where all young people are able to fully engage in learning and opportunities tied to their interests and passions, but we see the potential for online networks' playing a larger role in making this happen. Our decision to focus on practices and communities that embody this potential comes from our commitment to engaged scholarship. This book is an effort to make this potential more visible to educators, parents, and policy and technology makers who are seeking to expand educational opportunity. Our approach is animated by challenges that educators and technology designers face, and in turn, our findings are targeted toward insights that can be of value to researchers as well as practitioners. We orient our questions and methods to problems in practice as much as to scholarly debates.

We ask questions that social scientists have asked of social networks more generally, keyed to problems in educational practice. How do relationships and networks provide social support, information, and connections to opportunity? We probe more specifically into questions of learning and affinity. What kinds of relationships and networks support connected learning? Can online affinity networks help develop social capital, learning, and opportunity? And finally, what kinds of additional relationships and supports do young people need to connect their learning in affinity networks to academic, civic, and career opportunities?

Affinity networks provide a lens through which to deepen our understanding of social networks and learning. Our analysis pivots around how online affinity networks open unique avenues for young people to find "their people"—peers and mentors who share an identity or interest. While sharing similarities with other hobby and sports groups, the relationships that young people develop in online affinity networks differ in important ways from those developed through families, in schools, and in extracurricular activities. They are both more limited—tailored to bonding around a specific interest—and more expansive—

more accessible across time and space. They are "intentional" or chosen networks that can result in a strong sense of affiliation and social bonding. These networks are not layered with the same status hierarchies as young people's school peer culture, or the accountabilities of teachers and parents. Young people described this aspect of online affinity networks as liberating. Conversely, this means that these networks are thin along measures we traditionally associate with strong social ties, such as face-to-face interaction and institutional embeddedness. The intentional and self-contained aspects of affinity networks are also the features that limit their ability to connect to broader learning and civic and career opportunities. Investigating youth online affinity networks enables us understand how online networks are changing how young people shape their social relationships, identities, and learning in ways that inform educational practice.

After introducing the broader social, cultural, and economic climate that frames the agenda for this research, we describe the research study. We then describe the conceptual framework for this work and how it organizes the chapters to follow.

The Problem: Technology, Learning, and Equity

In the past decade, as young people have flocked to social media, mobile phones, and digital media of various kinds, we have seen a dramatic rise in media engagement and mediated communication. Between 1999 and 2015, the average number of hours that youth between the ages of 8 and 18 spent a day using media rose from 7.29 to 9 hours (Common Sense Media 2015). This rise in media engagement has led to concerns about the loss of reflective thought and cognition (Carr 2010), the rise of loneliness (Turkle 2011), declining standards of literacy (Bauerlein 2008), and media addiction. By contrast, proponents of digital learning have argued that these new technologies offer rich new opportunities for learning. Many have argued for the value of particular tools and technologies, such as gaming (McGonigal 2011; Prensky 2010), personalized learning systems, learning analytics, and open online content (Khan 2013).

Both proponents and detractors often focus more on the technology and generalizations about youth than on the specific social, cultural, and institutional contexts of their uptake. Technologies and techniques, however, take on different characteristics depending on the cultural and social settings they are embedded in. History is replete with examples of how new learning technologies have been heralded as the answer to our educational problems, only to become incorporated within existing institutionalized practices in decidedly nontransformative ways (Cuban 2003; Ito 2009; Rafalow 2016). Even when they are deployed in free and open online settings, we find that new educational technologies tend to amplify existing inequity; the most highly educated are the most likely to adopt these new open-education opportunities (Carfagna 2014; Hansen and Reich 2015; Reich and Ito 2017). Institutionalized practices, in education, entertainment, and the emerging technology landscape, drive the ways in which young people adopt new technology in differentiated ways in their everyday lives.

These studies of educational technology deployment have argued that focusing on the promise of a particular technology, technique, or platform can deflect attention away from deeply rooted and institutionalized forms of stratification and cultural differences. In other words, *access to social, cultural, and economic capital, not access to technology, is what broadens opportunity.* This recognition on its own, however, does not guide the way to positive and equitable roles for technology in learning. Both proponents and critical scholars must focus less on pinning hope and blame on technology, and more on understanding and adapting institutionalized practices and policies, if we are truly concerned about better and more equitable educational futures. The connected learning approach is an effort to move beyond a "boosters versus critics" divide through a shared agenda informed by both critical empirical studies of learning technology and forward-looking theories of change.

A shared progressive agenda for technology and learning is particularly important as informal learning and social networks play an increasingly important role in structuring opportunity for young people growing up in the United States and the Global North. Young people growing up in educated and economically stable families are enjoying a growing abundance of riches in learning opportunities. Not only are they likely to be attending a school that takes full advantage of new technology-enhanced learning, but their parents are spending unprecedented amounts of money on out-of-school enrichment activities. The economic investment of the wealthiest quintile of families has tripled to nearly $9,000 annually

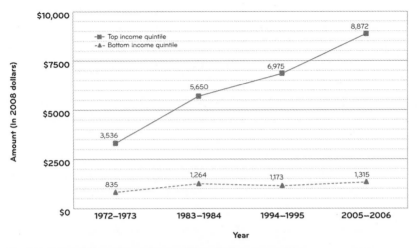

Figure 1.1. Growth in enrichment expenditures by income quintile.

Source: Duncan, Greg J., and Richard Murnane. Figure 1.6, "Enrichment Expenditures on Children, 1972–2006." In *Whither Opportunity? Rising Inequality, Schools, and Children's Life Chances.* © 2011 Russell Sage Foundation, 112 East 64th Street, New York, NY 10065. Reprinted with permission. https://www.russellsage.org/publications/whither-opportunity.

since the 1970s, while the poorest quintile of families' investments have continued to hover at about $1,000 annually during these same decades (Duncan and Murnane 2011; see figure 1.1). With the aid of online platforms, privileged and tech-savvy families are more effectively tapping their social networks to guide their children's specialized interests, cultivate career opportunities, and develop agency and voice. These out-of-school learning experiences and social connections are particularly important for success in high-tech sectors that put greater emphasis on innovation, problem solving, and hands-on learning (Thomas and Brown 2011; Wagner 2012).

The growth of these enrichment gaps argues for investigation into the *specifics* of technologies' intersection with existing forms of stratification, the variation in how young people engage and learn online, and what our learning institutions can do to address these differences. Why do some young people go online primarily to hang out with existing peers and to browse entertaining YouTube videos, while others dive into online tutorials, courses, and communities of interest that drive more specialized forms of "geeking out" and social organizing? What role can educators, parents, peers, and the developers of online resources play in shaping these dynamics? What kinds of institutional practices, policies, and infrastructures can build stronger connections between youth interests and sites of opportunity, particularly for less privileged groups? What kinds of cultural barriers and assumptions inhibit or facilitate the building of these connections? Only by asking these questions and gaining a greater grasp of how digital learning opportunities intersect with social, cultural, and economic differences can we begin to shape a progressive educational reform agenda keyed to today's networked world. This book addresses these questions by taking an in-depth look at online affinity networks and how they are connected and disconnected to educational, career, and civic opportunity. We turn now to a discussion of our research and case studies before concluding this introduction with the theoretical and conceptual framing for the chapters to follow.

Situating Our Research

The Leveling Up study, situated within an evolving arc of research that has become more strategic and impact-focused through time, is one effort within a broader interdisciplinary and collaborative network of research and practice. Here we describe this broader context in relation to our ongoing research and our collaborative network before turning to the specifics of how the case studies were selected, developed, and analyzed.

An Evolving Research Agenda

The Leveling Up project, part of the MacArthur Foundation's Digital Media and Learning (DML) Initiative and Connected Learning Research Network (CLRN), continues a line of ethnographic inquiry that the DML Initiative has supported since 2005. This research builds on Ito's prior, more exploratory and descriptive research in the Digital Youth Project, which conducted fieldwork between 2006 and 2007, when teens were flocking to MySpace, when YouTube was just taking off, and before the mobile internet and texting had taken hold in the United States. The Digital Youth Project is the largest ethnographic study of youth new media practices to date, involving 27 researchers, more than 800 interviews, and 5,000 hours of online observation. The study involved a broad scan of youth new media practices, asking foundational questions about how these technologies intersected with peer and romantic relations, family life, creative expression, work, and play. The book that resulted from the Digital Youth Project, *Hanging Out, Messing Around, and Geeking Out* (Ito et al. 2010), was not designed to directly inform educational practice or design. Nonetheless, we were heartened to see how the book inspired educators and designers to create programs and spaces that centered on youth culture and practices (Hernandez and Marroquin 2013; Larson et al. 2013; Seelye 2014).

The Digital Youth Project provided a baseline understanding of how young people are incorporating social media, digital games, and digital media into their everyday lives, but it was clear that more targeted inquiry was needed to inform design, policy, and other practical interventions. In particular, our findings about the highly uneven and often inequitable ways that new media opportunities were taken up gave us cause for concern. The interdisciplinary CLRN was launched in 2012 as an interlinked set of research projects that investigated, from different dimensions and with different methods, the challenges and opportunities in leveraging new media for progressive and equitable learning. Within the CLRN's range of projects, the Leveling Up study followed in the footsteps of the Digital Youth Project in continuing in-depth ethnographic investigation of youth new media practices, but with a focus on groups and practices that helped us understand and expand the potential of online networks to support connected learning.

The Leveling Up study represented a different moment in our research priorities, reflecting how new media have spread through various institutions and populations. A growing number of studies were investigating youth new media practices (Black 2008; boyd 2014; Clark 2013; Gee and Hayes 2010; Lange 2007; Watkins 2009), offering a firm base of empirical research. Facebook had taken over as the social media platform of choice, people of all ages had embraced online media for both work and play, and billion-dollar enterprises were going public as a result of these trends. The spread of new media into mainstream life and institutions meant that the online world was no longer just a haven for young people, as we saw in the early years of youth new media adoption, and that online networks and communities were splintering and differentiating in new and unexpected ways. This large-scale adoption of new media created an imperative to investigate the potential connections between young people's online activities and meaningful opportunities in education, civic institutions, and careers. The rapid incorporation of online networks into civic institutions and commercial enterprises lent urgency to the need for a positive agenda for engaging with youth new media practices.

The aim of the Leveling Up study was to provide in-depth empirical case studies of youth new media practices that could inform policy and design. This goal was fundamentally different from that of the earlier Digital Youth Project research, which sought to decode the underlying patterns of youth new media engagement, what we called "genres of participation." The new focus on targeted investigation of practices that enhance learning and equity is motivated by the urgency of informing the design and deployment of learning technologies and related programs. As we describe in more detail below, we selected exemplary and exceptional cases that demonstrate how connected learning can support diverse youth interests and learning.

This book combines empirical social scientific inquiry with a social change agenda that advocates for a specific orientation to learning and design. It is an effort at engaged scholarship grounded in evidence and social scientific inquiry, but undertaken in the service of improving the lives of young people from all walks of life. The study does not seek to be representative of youth online affinity networks, nor is it designed to critique gaps and pitfalls of these online networks, though we see value in and allies in both of these forms of inquiry. Critique of existing practices is necessary but not sufficient; we believe that those of us practicing ethnography and social science also have a role to play in presenting alternatives. At times this means we adopt a voice that is more oriented to design and advocacy than traditional scholarly social scientific discourse, but throughout the book we situate our claims and the nature of our analysis. The study is also situated within our broader interdisciplinary network, which includes a range of approaches and scholarly voices, including critical ethnography, survey research, and design research.

Nodes in a Collaborative Network

The Leveling Up project is part of the broader research agenda of the CLRN, which investigates both the pitfalls and promises of the connected learning agenda. Some CLRN studies conduct research on educator-guided and DML-supported programs explicitly designed to support connected learning (Arum et al., forthcoming; Ching et al. 2015; Larson et al. 2013; Penuel et al. 2015). Other studies investigate a wider range of educational programs in terms of principles of connected learning (Ben-Eliyahu, Rhodes, and Scales 2014; Van Horne et al. 2016). Yet another set of studies looks at settings that are quite distant from the aspirational model of connected learning to identify blind spots and the limits of the model (Livingstone and Sefton-Green 2016; Watkins et al. forthcoming). By focusing on youth-centered online environments with connected learning features, the Leveling Up cases sit between studies centered on environments explicitly designed to support connected learning and studies of more typical environments for youth learning and media engagement.

This book draws from fieldwork and case studies developed by CLRN researchers and researchers from the Youth and Participatory Politics Research Network (YPP). Unlike a more typical edited collection of ethnographic cases, our chapters are written based on cross-case analysis, analyzing themes and topics that have emerged across projects led by different researchers. Findings from individual cases have been published elsewhere (Korobkova 2014; Kow, Young, and Salen Tekinbaş 2014; Martin 2014; Pfister 2014; Rafalow and Salen Tekinbaş 2014), as have analyses of our data in relation to specific disciplinary debates (Martin 2016; Pfister 2016; Rafalow 2015; Ito et al. 2018). Readers of this book are introduced to each online affinity network and an exemplary learner in case summaries interspersed throughout, written by the researchers who led on the individual cases. The core chapters pull findings and patterns together to synthesize the empirical findings, theoretical contributions, and implications for practice across the cases. This format is an effort to provide context for each case while also surfacing cross-cutting patterns.

Researchers from the Leveling Up project have collaborated to take the role of lead author for the chapters, drawing material from varied case studies and researchers. This is a co-authored volume rather than an edited collection of work by individual contributors. This orientation to co-authorship and joint analysis aligns with a commitment to collaborative and interdisciplinary analysis that the MacArthur Foundation's DML Initiative has embraced for more than a decade. By funding two research networks, other major research projects, and infrastructures for collaboration, the DML Initiative has nurtured research that draws from a varied qualitative corpus and collaboration with quantitative researchers. This book is one among many efforts in the initiative to synthesize findings across varied research projects, with a specific focus on cross-case analysis of in-depth qualitative research in networked settings.

When examining networked forms of culture and social behavior, researchers have struggled to define research settings that involve networks of both local and more far-flung relationships. Ethnographic researchers have tended to reproduce many of the characteristics of traditional ethnography within online spaces by focusing on communities that enable "deep hanging out" and on the development of strong social ties and shared practices (Geertz 1998). These have included studies of massively multiplayer online games (MMOs) (Nardi 2010; Taylor 2009), virtual worlds (Boellstorff 2008; Kendall 2002), and specialized online forums (Baym 2000; Hine 2000) that are conducted primarily or exclusively online. Other researchers have pursued a hybrid approach that includes online observations and interviews, as well as participation in physical gatherings and sampling through local communities. For example, in her study of social media use, danah boyd traveled to different parts of the country to interview youth about their social media use rather than recruiting through online means (boyd 2014). In Ito's study of anime fans, she recruited through both specialized online communities and local fan events (Ito 2012a, 2012b). All of these approaches dip into the stream of highly fluid and networked forms of youth activity that span physical and networked spaces, relationships, and practices.

The collaborative research context of the DML research projects and networks offered an opportunity to take a different approach, to develop a linked set of ethnographic case studies that strategically sample from different populations and forms of social organization. We combine the strengths of in-depth, observational, and contextually attuned case research with a comparative analysis that surfaces patterns and relationships between and within cases. We developed a set of shared protocols so that all the case studies had a common bank of interview and survey questions and shared codes, using both a priori and emergent coding.[1] This cultural and practice-based analysis is still interpretive and qualitative in nature, and it does not rest on the kinds of sampling approaches and claims for representativeness characteristic of quantitative research. But it does offer a way of analyzing patterns of social organization and cultural forms that synthesizes across conventional case-based research. It is a form of qualitative "meta-analysis" that draws findings from across varied case research that has asked similar questions.

Case Studies

The Leveling Up project began in fall 2011, with the majority of the fieldwork taking place in 2012 and 2013. The cases include a variety of affinity networks that make use of online spaces, and they employed research methods varying from questionnaires, surveys, semistructured interviews, observation, and content analyses of media, profiles, videos, and other online artifacts.[2] When we present ethnographic research in this book, we indicate which of the case studies the example is drawn from. To acknowledge young people as agents, we use the pseudonyms and ethnic and racial categories that our interviewees used to describe themselves. More on each of the case studies can be found in the individual case narratives that punctuate this book. The analysis this book is drawn from includes five case studies conducted as part of the Leveling Up study. We also draw from three other complementary cases of online affinity networks that were conducted as part of other research studies.

- Ksenia Korobkova's *One Direction fanfiction* case study delved into an online fanfiction community, members of which are connected to each other in two ways: (1) with an online forum and other media outlets, and (2) through *Directioner* fan art.
- The *Ravelry.com* case study, led by Rachel Cody Pfister, examined an online community and database for fiber crafting (knitting, crocheting, weaving, and spinning). The research focused on *Hogwarts at Ravelry*, an interest group that combines the interests of *Harry Potter* and fiber crafting to create a fictional universe.

- Two gaming case studies examined the creative culture and practices among both players and industry game developers engaged with *Little-BigPlanet 2* and *StarCraft II*. Adam Ingram-Goble, Matthew H. Rafalow, Yong Ming Kow, Katie Salen, and Timothy Young collaborated on these two case studies.
- The *professional wrestling fandom* case study, led by Crystle Martin, examined fan communities of professional wrestling, with a focus on fantasy wrestling through role-playing narratives.
- The *anime music video (AMV) community* is a case study conducted by Mizuko Ito as part of the earlier Digital Youth Project, and it focuses on a subcommunity of English-language fans of Japanese anime who create and share remixed videos.
- The *Nerdfighter* case study, led by Neta Kligler-Vilenchik, is based on research from the Media, Activism, and Participatory Politics (MAPP) project led by Henry Jenkins at USC and part of the YPP network. It centers on an informal community formed around the YouTube vlog channel for brothers John and Hank Green. Many of the participants are high school and college age, united by a shared identity as "nerds" and a broad common goal of "decreasing World Suck."
- The *Bollywood dance* case study builds on Sangita Shresthova's decade-long research on live Bollywood dance communities. This case study explores Bollywood dance as a participatory interest-driven practice in the United States as it delves into the Hindi Film Dance (HFC) competition scene on college campuses.

In selecting the cases, we were inspired by the "positive deviance" approach developed in the context of public health, which seeks out examples of practices already existing in communities that can be spread and scaled to address systemic problems (Pascale, Sternin, and Sternin 2010). We sought out affinity networks that exhibited dimensions of connected learning; they all include a focus on knowledge, expertise, and excellence, and they embody a set of community norms, values, and practices that support this orientation. All of these affinity networks also enable connections to academic, civic, and future opportunity for at least some of the participants. Finally, these groups also leverage digital media in effective ways, supporting more diverse forms of creative production and voice and making their affinity networks accessible to more participants.

In addition to seeking positive deviants to inform and support the spread of connected learning experiences, case selection was motivated by the equity agenda of connected learning. In developing our case studies, we not only sought high-functioning affinity networks, but we also sought out areas of interest that catered to diverse populations, particularly those groups underrepresented in technology fields, specifically girls and black and Latino youth. The majority of research on affinity networks to date has focused on groups that are stereotypically geeky and tech savvy. Today's online world, particularly if we consider mobile, social, and entertainment media, crosses lines of class, gender, and race, and we thought it was critically important to gain a deeper understanding of how connected learning opportunities can reach populations who have, until recently, been more at the "digital edge" (Watkins et al., forthcoming).

Several of our case studies focus on what might be considered the dominant culture of digital elites, chosen in order to gain an understanding of online affinity networks pushing technological innovation. Online gaming communities have historically led in innovation of networked learning practices and peer production. The case studies of *StarCraft II* and *LittleBigPlanet 2* represent this technological cutting edge, showcasing the state of the art in game development, networked community organization, and peer production. These studies, along with the Ravelry case, also highlight the often hidden partner in connected learning experiences—the designers and developers behind the online platforms that youth are using. The coupling is tight between developers and players in the game industry, and game developers often see a core focus of their work as the design of dynamic learning communities, rather than just the games themselves. The AMV case also represents a highly tech-savvy group, dominated by white and Asian young men. The case study of the *Nerdfighters*, from the MAPP project, describes a digitally activated geek community of predominantly young women that has pushed innovation in civic activism through digital networks.

Four of our case studies were selected specifically because they were not characteristic of the stereotypically geeky cultures dominated by white and Asian young men. We arrived at our case study of professional wrestling fans after extensive exploration into affinity networks of youth historically underrepresented in online affinity networks. Many affinity networks that are popular among black and Latino youth, such as those around sports games or music, were ruled out because we could not find a robust online-community component. Unlike these popular practices that have high status among youth, however, professional wrestling is often stigmatized in local peer groups, and fans are driven to online forums and sociability to cement their affinity networks. To further diversify the populations of youth we were engaged with, we invited an additional case study of the Bollywood dance scene from Shresthova, a member of the MAPP team. The Bollywood case rounds out our range of interest areas in providing an example of a highly digitally activated group, this one centered on young South Asians. Two other cases were selected because of their appeal to women and girls. The case study of the One Direction (1D) fanfiction affinity network taps into the energies of one of the most activated and mainstream fandoms for younger teenage girls. Ravelry represents an older age set, and it has enabled us to look at intergenerational connections through an interest area that has stood the test of time.

The intergenerational nature of the knitting scene relates to a final and crucial point of differentiation in our cases. The interest areas differed widely in the degree to which they provided a point of intergenerational connection or disconnection and in how culturally distant they were from educational, civic, and career-relevant spheres. The 1D case study represented one end of this spectrum, with a high degree of cultural disconnect between what adults and educators and the youth participants found valuable. It is an interest area that tends not to be culturally valued outside of the affinity network and is likely to elicit eye rolls from parents and educators. By contrast, despite being stigmatized by more mainstream and elite populations, professional wrestling proved to be a point of intergenerational connection in families, and with some educators. Our cases were selected because we thought they afforded opportunities for connected learning across settings, so the other cases, to varying degrees, all provided openings for the kinds of intergenerational and cross-sector brokering we saw with the professional wrestling case. We excluded many popular youth interests—such as first-person shooters—from consideration because we thought that there was insurmountable distance between the culture of the affinity network and educational settings. In all of the case studies, we see the need for a set of supporting points of translation and brokering that connects the spheres of play and learning, and youth and adult worlds, in order to realize connected learning. Our cases to varying degrees exemplify both these disconnects and cultural distance but skew toward those that can potentially connect across these divides.

Our focus on positive deviants has meant that our analysis excludes many important dimensions of youth participation in online affinity networks. Our focus on high-functioning affinity networks means that our groups are less likely to exhibit negative social dynamics such as hate, overt conflict, and self-harm. In addition, our research subjects tend toward the central and successful members of these networks, who are most likely to experience connected learning. We have little understanding of those who are excluded, drop out, or participate casually. This results from our focus on connected learners, as well as the fact that we observed and recruited within the affinity networks themselves, rather than recruiting a more representative sample of youth through community organizations or schools. These blind spots were unavoidable outcomes of the aim of this study, which was targeted toward surfacing how features of online affinity networks could guide design and positive social change. While many of the dynamics that we describe are common across varied online affinity networks, we signal throughout the text the uniqueness of the examples in this book and when the dynamics are likely more specific to the positive examples we sought out. We also point out when we do have visibility into negative dynamics such as exclusion and conflict. For example, chapter 3 examines status dynamics and hierarchies in the affinity networks we studied. We suggest that readers look to other studies to understand the realities of young people who are less connected to the types of online affinity networks that are the subject of our study.[3]

What our cases offer is a window into common characteristics of online affinity networks that *do* support connected learning. These include strongly shared culture and practices, varied ways of contributing, high standards, and effective ways of providing feedback and help. Unlike much of the learning that young people encounter in school, affinity networks provide opportunities that are self-selected and intentional, and that are also tied to contributions to social communities and authentic recognition in these communities. This can involve being a community organizer, publishing work online, competing in a public tournament, and providing feedback and expertise for others. Young people have historically had these kinds of opportunities for learning, contribution, and recognition in adult-sponsored athletics and the arts; the online world can make these kinds of opportunities more varied, accessible, and youth driven.

How Affinity Networks Connect Interests to Learning

The learning sciences have increasingly recognized the role of culture, social relationships, and shared practice in the discovery of interests and persistence in pursuing them.[4] Research on the development of interests has documented how familial support (Crowley et al. 2015; Crowley and Jacobs 2002), the availability of shared activities (Azevedo 2011, 2013), and rapport with teachers and mentors (Maltese and Tai 2010) play a more significant role than formal instruction in the development of scientific interests. Our research on young people and affinity networks reinforces these views of interest development. We draw from Azevedo's view that interests are an interaction between individual preferences and "lines of practice"—the ways in which interests are sustained over time through joint activities. We see an ongoing and dynamic interaction between individual inclinations and the network of relationships, affinities, and activities that are available in a young person's social world. Even when young people have a strong personal passion for a particular interest area, involvement waxes and wanes depending on whether they feel a sense of belonging, if they have friends, family members, and mentors who share the interest, and on access to activities that sustain their involvement. We describe young people's personal predilection for an interest as an "affinity" in order to highlight its relational and culturally situated nature. A young person's demonstration of interest is grounded in personal preference as well as whether he or she can relate to the culture, people, and practices that embody the interest. Whether it is math, surfing, or knitting, an interest cannot be separated from its culture, people, and places. These contextual features are fundamental drivers of young people's attraction to the area of interest.

We see our work on sociocultural contexts for interest development as complementary to psychological research that investigates how interest is triggered, sustained, and deepened (e.g., Renninger and Hidi 2016). We see deepening interest as both "internally" developmental and as an "external" process of building connections that are relational, cultural, and practical in nature. In other words, robust interest is not a process of "internalization" and is characterized by growth in situational ties; the focus of our investigation has been the development of these sociocultural ties and networks. In this we draw from a long tradition in sociocultural learning theory that recognizes how learning is part of belonging in situated practices (e.g., Brown, Collins, and Duguid 1989; Cole 1996; Lave and Wenger 1991). Unlike the seminal case studies of situated learning in professional "communities of practice" (Lave and Wenger 1991; Orr 1990; Wenger 1998), however, our cases center on networks of affinity and interests that are only loosely institutionalized. We draw broadly on sociocultural approaches in the learning sciences, but we focus specifically on the unique forms of social learning that thrive in technology-enabled affinity networks.

Growing out of sociocultural research traditions, connected learning also draws from learner-centered and socially situated approaches to educational practice. At least since John Dewey (1916) articulated a vision for progressive educational practice that connects school and community, educators have sought to support meaningful, hands-on learning that connects young people to the wider world. The connected learning model draws from this progressive tradition, situating it within today's challenges of equity, inclusion, and a changing media environment. Connected learning sees common cause with hands-on and experiential approaches such as project-based learning, inquiry-based learning, and constructionism (Papert 1993), in addition to affinities with culturally relevant approaches (e.g., González, Moll, and Amanti 2005; Gutiérrez and Rogoff 2003) and critical pedagogy (Freire [1970] 2000). Connected learning is not limited, however, to a particular pedagogical approach. Instead, the focus is on building relational, practical, and conceptual connections across settings and experiences, centered on learning interests and affinities (see figures 1.2a and 1.2b). Often a project-centered and culturally relevant approach is the best way to build these connections.

If we return to the story of Amy that introduced this chapter, we can see that her process of developing interests and expertise relied on a growing network of relational supports, activities, and opportunities

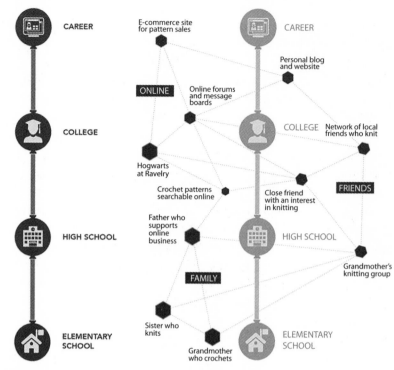

Figure 1.2a. Learning and interest development as a pipeline or progression. Image by Nat Soti.

Figure 1.2b. Learning and interest development as a process of network building. Image by Nat Soti.

to share. Her online affinity network in *Hogwarts at Ravelry* helped fill gaps in knowledge, as well as in her social and cultural supports, so that she could sustain her learning and interest in a unique specialization. Unlike an interest such as chess or basketball, which is often supported within schools and other community-based institutions, a specialization in knitting and pattern making would have been difficult to sustain without her online supports.

The fundamental drivers of specialized, expert learning are the same as what we see in more traditional professional groups—learning in situ, sustained engagement with peers with related expertise, and productive social and cultural contributions. What differs is how Amy's interests are supported through an online, affinity-centered infrastructure that is only loosely institutionalized. Online affinity networks are more

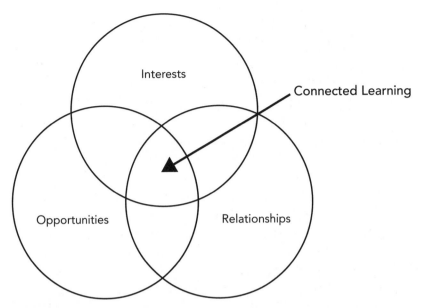

Figure 1.3. Connecting the spheres of learning.
Image by Mizuko Ito.

accessible than a formal professional community or a community-based organization such as a sports team. This also means, however, that they have fewer ties to the local communities and contexts of participants. In Amy's case, her supportive family provided these connections, thus enabling a connected learning experience that linked her online and face-to-face settings. Our case studies of online affinity networks and connected learners such as Amy enable us to understand these unique affordances of the online world as well as to reflect on our assumptions about learning and interest development.

The chapters of this book are sequenced to trace how young people get involved in online affinity networks, find a place for themselves in the social scene, and connect those experiences and that learning to academic, civic, and career opportunities. This arc is not so much a learning trajectory as much as it is a map of how online affinity networks can fit into a network of learning activities and relationships centered on youth interests. Although there are steps and pathways that young people traverse through time, connected learning is more appropriately conceived of as the growth of a network of connections than as a linear pathway or an internalization of skills and knowledge. Connected learners are situated within a set of personal and organizational relationships that knit together their interests and affinities, relationships, and organizational sites of power and opportunity such as schools, civic institutions, and workplaces (see figure 1.3).

Online affinity networks can play a powerful role in connecting a young person's learning network because they distill and make accessible a set of relationships and roles that are centered on personal interests and identities. For young people who do not have peers and mentors in their local communities and organizations that share their interest, online affinity networks can fill a vacuum in their connected learning networks. And when they are able to connect the relationships and learning from their online affinity networks back to their local relationships and organizations, the outcomes can be transformational—opening new educational pathways, civic engagements, and economic opportunity. The chapters in this book take on these three dimensions of the network of connected learning by first describing the interests and shared practices that draw young people into online affinity networks, and then turning to the dynamics of peer status that they encounter when they are engaged in these communities. The final chapter looks at links from online affinity networks to academic, economic, and civic opportunity. The organization of the chapters also mirrors the interdisciplinary nature of this study, which brings together internet studies, social network analysis, and the learning sciences. Each chapter highlights the contributions that a study of online affinity networks can make to each of these fields of study in turn.

Interests and Affinity

In the second chapter of this book, we delve into the core practices and structures that make online affinity networks tick: how they wrap themselves around a shared "content world" (Jenkins 2012), organize shared practices that engage participants, and build open online infrastructures that welcome new participants and challenge veterans. We draw from prior research on participatory culture and online communities of interest (Gee and Hayes 2010; Jenkins 1992; Jenkins et al. 2009) and consider the unique forms of social bonding that young people encounter in online affinity networks. The practices we describe are situated within a trend that internet researchers have identified for people to increasingly leverage mobile and online technology to build more intentional and specialized networks (Lenhart et al. 2015; Matsuda 2005; Rainie and Wellman 2012).

Depending on the interest, the glue that holds online affinity networks together varies widely. Competition and tournaments are the shared purpose that drives the *StarCraft* affinity network. For young people who knit and create levels in *LittleBigPlanet*, creative challenges are a focal point for the community. Bollywood dancers orchestrate performances, and *Nerdfighters* mobilize around social causes. While united by a shared content world, infrastructure, and affinity, successful online affinity networks are spaces of constant renewal. Moderators and community leaders describe a process of constant adaptation in order to continue to respond to an ever-changing network and sustain engagement. What are the cultural content, shared activities, and infrastructures that hold these networks together, and how do they adapt through time?

In addition to describing the infrastructure, culture, and shared practices that hold an online affinity network together, this chapter also considers the role that networks that are learning centered can play in young people's discovering new interests and deepening existing ones. The chapter locates the online affinity networks we studied as a particular kind of influence in young people's lives, one that enables them to connect to specialized knowledge and relationships that are not present in their homes and local organizations. Young people take to online affinity networks when they want to embrace interests and affiliations that parents and teachers think are a waste of time and that are stigmatized by their local peer groups. One Direction and professional wrestling fans describe how online fandoms offered a safe space for them to geek out on interests that many in their local communities looked down on, and *StarCraft* players hid their obsession with the game from their parents. Even in cases such as knitting, in which the interest has a positive or neutral valence in the family or with local peers, young people describe the online affinity networks as a place where they were able to connect with people who really "get" them and understand the passion they bring to their interest.

Peer Status and Social Capital

Online affinity networks are a context where young people can form social relationships and networks that differ from those they find in their schools, sports, and local communities. Chapter 3 takes up questions of how status and reputation are negotiated in online affinity networks, and the forms of social capital that young people gain from affinity-based relationships they develop in these networks. Online affinity networks that are learning centered give young people a context to be recognized for creative production, specialized knowledge, and commitments to a community or cause. These pursuits can also be sequestered from their everyday identities in school and in families, which can give them a safe space of experimentation and expression, supported by peers who really "get it" and have a shared appreciation for their commitments. Because they rely on open online infrastructures, online affinity networks can have low barriers to entry, and those we examined embrace a welcoming and inclusive ethos. At the same time, when they are focused on high-quality work and performance, they develop social processes for recognizing achievement and contributions to the community that create status distinctions. How do learning-oriented online affinity networks mark achievement, contributions, and status in the network? What kinds of social support and benefits come with young people's gaining status in these networks?

The relationships that young people develop in online affinity networks can be strong and intimate because of the shared affinity and camaraderie of these settings. At the same time, they also have qualities of what Mario Small has described as "compartmentalized intimates"— relationships that are strong but tied to very specific activities and affiliations (Small 2009). The knowledge, skills, status, and social capital that young people develop in online affinity networks are highly valued within the interest group, but they often do not connect and translate beyond those who are in this network. It is akin to what Sarah Thornton has described as "subcultural capital" in describing the indie music clubbing scene (Thornton 1996). Being set off from mainstream culture and organizations creates a strong sense of belonging and unique markers of status, which simultaneously creates boundaries that inhibit connection to social and cultural capital outside of the affinity network. Our cases have varying degrees of tension with the cultural and social status markers of adult and mainstream institutions, but they are all characterized by robust internal markers of reputation, achievement, and status.

Opportunity: Connecting Back to the Wider World

After examining the characteristics of peer status and reputation, the book then takes the final step in the journey through the connected learning model. How and when do the learning and social capital developed in online affinity networks connect and translate to academic, civic, and career opportunities? In many ways, the strength of the bonding and learning that happen in online affinity networks is grounded in their relative independence from the status hierarchies that characterize local peer networks and the more goal-directed learning and achievement of résumé building for school and career. At the same time, we observed instances of young people's leveraging the learning and relationships developed in their online affinity networks in the wider world.

These connections were most seamlessly developed for groups centered on a "connected civics" model, in which the interest and affinity are already centered on real-world activism and civic action (Ito et al. 2015). In other cases, young people applied skills they developed—such as mathematical reasoning or writing—to in-school settings. We also found examples of young people's parlaying their online activities into immediate economic benefits—such as selling knitting patterns online—as well as longer-term career pathways—such as choosing to pursue vocational training related to the interest area.

These examples point to the ways in which we can frame educational supports in terms of brokering and connection building rather than the more conventional notion of "transfer." The ability of young people to make these connections from affinity networks to opportunity were not simply about the individual's "applying" or "generalizing" knowledge and skills but rested on very specific relational, infrastructural, and organizational supports such as a close relationship to a teacher, a school offering, or civic action related to an interest.

In the final chapter of the book, we explicitly explore the implications of our research for educational practice and the design of programs and technology. While online affinity networks may not be explicitly designed to support connected learning, they provide a rich set of lessons for those seeking to leverage the emerging affordances of the online world in the service of learning that is engaged, equitable, and meaningful.

The *Wrestling Boards*

Crystle Martin

The wrestlers wait with bated breath for the unveiling of the match card, which tells players whom they will be wrestling that week.[1] As soon as the match card is released by the booker, who manages the fantasy wrestling federation, the wrestlers gleefully spring into action—creating feuds with the wrestler or wrestlers they are paired with that week. Throughout the course of the week, the wrestlers build and perfect their feuds—creating written, audio, or video promos about how they are going to win their match against the opposing wrestler (see figure C.1.1.). At the end of a given week, the booker calls a halt to the feuding, and the anticipation grows as three writers launch into a frenzied weekend of activity, in which they churn out up to 85 pages of text. These stories are released to the wrestlers, who devour every moment—from the time the first wrestler hits the ramp to the last move of the last match with a winner being declared—and every scrap of text between. The wrestlers enjoy every moment of the narrative of the match that grew out of their carefully crafted and raucous feuds. The wrestlers discuss the match and share praise and criticism with the writers, and then the whole process begins again with a new match card and new feuds.

Professional wrestling traces its roots to the nineteenth century (*Scientific American* 1895) and has thrived as a major pastime in North America for the past four decades. World Wrestling Entertainment (or WWE) is now the largest professional wrestling promotion group in the world. Professional wrestling, with its focus on dramatic performance, differs markedly from the ancient Greek–influenced sport of amateur wrestling seen in the Olympics and in collegiate settings. Despite professional wrestling's popularity, being a fan continues to carry a cultural stigma and is seen as decidedly lowbrow, much like video games (Sammond 2005). Outsiders often object to the vulgar nature of both and see

Figure C.1.1. A wrestling card created by a fantasy wrestling federation participant and the booker.

Image courtesy of Rhashan.

them as educational wastelands devoid of cultural value. But just like the varied genres of video game entertainment, professional wrestling offers participants a variety of educational and culturally relevant experiences. The WWE alone has more than 220 million members on its social media network, with local-language websites in 23 countries (WWE, n.d.).

Founded in 2011 by administrator Crayo, a 19-year-old white male from the United Kingdom, the *Wrestling Boards* is an online professional wrestling community where wrestling fans come together in a supportive space to share and explore their interest. On the *Wrestling Boards*, participants discuss many aspects of the sport and their surrounding interests, and participate in the community's fantasy wrestling federation (FWF) *Over the Ropes*, which is essentially a text-based role-playing game. This is a space where the love of professional wrestling intermingles with an enjoyment of role-playing and writing.

Participants on the site range in age from 15 to older than 60, with the majority falling in the 16 to 25 range. A majority of participants are male, although the community has several very active female members in its core community. The *Wrestling Boards* forum has more than 4,300 members, but only about 100 participate in the FWF, with about 20 characters participating in a season of matches at a time. Despite its smaller number of participants, the FWF is a vibrant and active part of the forums.

The *Wrestling Boards* forums are very user friendly, allowing participants to add elaborate signature images or .gifs, mashups of their favorite wrestler(s), or in one participant's case, a mashup of his favorite wrestler and his favorite *My Little Pony* character from the newest version of the television show. Community members frequently include links to outside resources, videos, and audio files so that they can share news, opinions, best-of videos, and a host of other information with others on the forum about the complex story lines surrounding professional wrestling. They also participate in a variety of shared activities within the fantasy wrestling federation, such as feuding in character and writing reviews of each week's show.

Participants in the community describe again and again the importance of help and feedback to the community, and supporting each other is a shared expectation among members. In the professional wrestling fandom, educating newcomers about "the product" of wrestling is a shared goal of the community. Some new fans believe that wrestling is a real sport, and wrestling fans work hard to educate these "marks" into what Crayo calls "smarks," helping them to understand that professional wrestling is scripted and choreographed and is actually a genre of television writing. Participants on the *Wrestling Boards* answer each other's questions about wrestling story lines, wrestlers, wrestling history, community norms, and participating in the fantasy wrestling federation.

They use help and feedback as a support system and as a way to create social bonds with other participants. Jonathan, a 16-year-old white male from the United Kingdom, describes why help and feedback are so prominent in the community: "At the end of the day, we're all alike and we're like a family on *Wrestling Boards*."

The site was just a year old when I first started observing it, so at the time the core group of original members was still very prominent in participation and visibility. These members have earned special status because of their history with the community. The site allows members of the community to have titles under their chosen image or avatar, which are given by specific groups or for actions on the forum. They can also display the trophies they earn for things such as "member of the month." Participants use a variety of strategies to determine who has status on the forum, including activity, quality of postings, trophies earned, and so on. Only rarely do they use the reputation system that is built into the forums; instead they use a system similar to the way people evaluate "likes" on a Facebook post.

Learner Story

The story of one *Wrestling Boards* participant illustrates how a lifelong interest can evolve into an avenue for expertise development and to a potential career path. Rhashan, a 19-year-old African American male from New Jersey, has been watching wrestling nearly his entire life. "I started watching when I was three or two years old because my mother had introduced it to me and I was automatically entertained." His initial introduction to wrestling was during the Attitude Era, a period of wrestling for the WWE—then the WWF—from the latter half of the 1990s to the early 2000s that was marked by a shift to more adult content. Rhashan has attended an extraordinary number of wrestling shows live: "3 house shows, 8 Raws, 4 Smackdowns, 2 Pay Per Views, and 4 Wrestlemanias." Despite his family's support of his interest, Rhashan has no local community to discuss wrestling with. "In my hometown there are scattered wrestling fans here and there, nothing intense for people my age. However, children seem to be all watching it." Because of this, Rhashan has become guarded about sharing his interest outside the *Wrestling Boards*. "Some of my friends have an interest in WWE and I've made friends on this site, but I don't know these guys in real life. I haven't introduced my friends to WWE. WWE is not something that's like amazing to show around, it's just something I like."

Through Rhashan's long history with wrestling, he has developed a detailed method that he uses to choose which wrestlers to support.

> Daniel Bryan is my favorite wrestler at the moment. I choose wrestlers to support based on who's not in the top tier, like Cena & CM Punk. I like to go for fresher guys and people who haven't gotten that shot yet. However that's the least important aspect. I think that a wrestler must, of course, be able to wrestle a good match, and I've seen some that can't. The last aspect is mic skills, which is the ability to captivate an audience just by using a mic. It seems worthless, but it's the mic that builds up the hype for every match.

His interest in the total package, including the theatricality of a wrestler's performance on the microphone, stems from his long history with wrestling, as well as from his interest in the creative pursuit of filmmaking and his understanding that it takes many elements to create a great dramatic scene.

Rhashan is an expert in his interest, with a long memory of its history, story lines, and wrestlers. If you ask him about his favorite wrestlers, you get answers that span a decade. He is also a heavy technology user when it comes to participating in his interest, using social media, YouTube, wrestling news sites, and forums. Rhashan has developed a web series on YouTube in which he creates analysis videos of the weekly show *RAW* and the annual pay-per-view event *WrestleMania*. He displays technical skill in video and audio editing, splicing together segments of the television broadcasts with shots of himself talking, and the audio runs seamlessly throughout each video. He enjoys the *Wrestling Boards* because it offers varied perspectives on wrestling through its diverse international community, and because it gives him access to a steady stream of people who are interested in his filmmaking. Rhashan uses his digital skills in video and audio editing to enhance his participation in *Over the Ropes*. "No one else really does *Over the Ropes* like I do, to the extent of shooting real promos." With feedback from the community, he improves his video scripts as well as his video and audio production. He thinks that the videography skills he is developing in the *Over the Ropes* role-playing community are helping him to hone his career in filmmaking. Rhashan is interested in building a larger following and connections to future opportunity, using the *Wrestling Boards* as a site to develop and launch his future career as a filmmaker.

StarCraft II

Yong Ming Kow, Amanda Wortman, and Timothy Young

You know your opponent is coming even before you can see his or her forces.[1] As soon as gameplay starts, you balance resource collection and unit creation to build your own army (as seen in figure C.1.2). Each decision you make has ramifications for the entire match and is made at the expense of something else. Did you build enough medics? What about base defense? The game is all about strategy and speed. Efficiency is the key. And just as in chess, different strategies can be employed to defeat your opponent. The strategies differ based on the map you are playing, the race you are competing against, and the play-style of your opponent. But like any good chess player, you go to the match with a variety of versatile strategies in your back pocket so you can change your strategy no matter what situation arises.

StarCraft II is one of the most popular PC-based real-time strategy games and is labeled by many of its participants as the chess of the 21st century. It is part of a franchise of games, with the first of its series, *StarCraft*, released by Blizzard Entertainment in 1998. *StarCraft*'s well-designed and balanced competitive gameplay encouraged droves of youth to pit their skills against each other, a practice that eventually became what is now known as esports, or the practice of regulated competition with video games. The population of *StarCraft II* gamers is fairly homogenous, consisting mostly of college and high school students, as well as a significant number of young working adults. The interviewees in our study ranged in age from 15 to 30 years old and were predominantly male, though we interviewed a handful of females. About 90 percent of our interviewees were either white or Asian American. In the early years, *StarCraft* events were mostly self-organized by youth interest groups. But in 2011 and 2012, these competitive events saw rapid

Figure C.1.2. A *StarCraft II* match tests players' ability to manage a battlefield in real time. Image courtesy of Blizzard Entertainment.

growth, with international tournaments awarding $2.5 million and $4 million, respectively, to winners.

The lore and backstory of the game flesh out an engaging and rich content world for players to explore during narrative-driven single-player games. In a *StarCraft II* competitive match, players control armies to engage in intergalactic warfare. The army units that players control, the maps that players compete on, and the art surrounding the world all contribute to the epic *StarCraft II* story line. Players control one of three factions—Terrans (human), Zerg (swarm insectoid creatures), or Protoss (futuristic alien race)—building bases, managing their economy, and raising an army to defeat their opponents. The game and community present a unique environment in which competition and professional play become a platform for self-directed learning and improvement, as well as inspiring various initiatives for community growth.

At the core of participants' discourses about *StarCraft II* is the "metagame," or "any planning, preparation, or maneuvering that a player does outside of actual gameplay to gain an advantage" (Team Liquid 2013b). In other words, it is the analysis of game mechanics and shifting social discourses of strategies within the community—which comes from deep analysis of high-level gameplay and active participation in online forums and video commentaries. While the metagame often refers more widely to any game-related activities that take place outside a game's formal play space (Salen and Zimmerman 2004), the term, as used by *StarCraft* players, captures the robust way in which the game connects shared purpose in an interest-driven activity to learning and expertise development around that activity.

Driven by a common interest in the metagame, *StarCraft II* players both consume and create a range of media content, such as videos and articles, which they often link to one or several of the *StarCraft* community hubs, such as Day[9]TV (day9.tv) or *Team Liquid* (teamliquid.net). Day[9]TV features web shows revolving around high-level analysis of *StarCraft* gameplay. Day[9]TV is extremely popular among community members for its mix of high-level strategy analysis, humor, and approachability for players of all levels. Other hubs, such as *Team Liquid*, have been built through the efforts of volunteer fans who contribute their time to write articles, produce videos, and organize online and offline events, such as tournaments. These practices demonstrate how a game such as *StarCraft II* can enable players to anchor their interests to develop strategic and systemic thinking as well as contribute to a community and shared culture.

Although *StarCraft II* supports single-player play, the dominant mode is highly social, with players competing and practicing with one another and also studying the play of others. Blizzard Entertainment provides an online matching system, called "the ladder," that players use to identify random practice partners. But players also take the initiative to seek out volunteer coaches and teachers in order to benefit from a more personal form of learning. Day[9]TV reflects this peer-supported ethos by hosting forums where players exchange knowledge and tips, allowing for community chat during the live shows, and inviting player suggestions for show content and contributions of game replays. While Sean Plott, a 25-year-old white male from California, is the personality and expert behind the show and the site, his approach and demeanor reflect a welcoming, unpretentious community ethos as he continuously seeks input and feedback from the crowd of *StarCraft* enthusiasts and experts.

StarCraft II is designed by Blizzard Entertainment so that players can get involved in content production, sharing, and curation. The *Team Liquid* online forum is an important participatory hub for these content producers. The site serves as a repository for various digital media such as articles, forum and wiki posts, and weblinks that cover a wide range of competition strategies. Apart from sharing core content related to the *StarCraft II* metagame, *Team Liquid* also acts as an information hub for the community where members publicize local activities to the rest of the community members. Younger players can also use *Team Liquid* to form open-membership and cross-generational practice partnerships so that they are exposed to more experienced players as personal coaches. According to a *Team Liquid* survey, 62 percent of its users are students, while 24 percent are employed full time (Team Liquid 2012).

Among all production activities, forum posting and article writing are perhaps the most accessible for players. New York–based Waxangel, in his early 20s and the team's chief editor, told us that writing is one sure way to get players involved in the community. Any *Team Liquid* participant can post to its forum, which is moderated only for offensive content. It also has a writing team. The only difference between general forum posters and *Team Liquid* writers is that the writing team tends to write longer articles and also receives peer support from Waxangel and his editorial team. Some of these articles analyze strategies, while others report on gaming events or introduce professional gamers.

Waxangel hand-picks his writers by inviting forum posters who exhibit relevant aptitude. He describes an important hallmark of a good *Team Liquid* writer as "someone who is very passionate at esports, because a guy who's not that good at writing technically but has a lot of passion for esports, you can definitely tell that in his writing." Waxangel welcomes writers such as Day[9], who already has an illustrious reputation in *StarCraft II*, to publish anytime.

Occasionally, *StarCraft II* gamers find career opportunities in professional gaming if they put in years of effort in learning and practicing with other equally dedicated players. Likewise, content producers who attain high levels of expertise in writing articles or broadcasting events may also find employment opportunities in the gaming industry. For example, the shows on Day[9]TV, which began as a passion project and online daily TV show devoted to the art and strategy of *StarCraft II*, became a full-time job for Sean Plott.

Learner Story

Mona Zhang is a 22-year-old Asian American college student at Princeton University and the female founder and leader of the *Collegiate Starleague*.[2] Mona is also a master level player, meaning that she is among the top 2 percent of players in the United States. Mona is both a powerful player and a community leader—a strong role model for other female gamers.

As with most active *StarCraft* participants, Mona's experience with computer games started at an early age. She first started playing *StarCraft* when she was 11 years old because her brother was playing it, and she wanted to do the same. Her relationship with her brother had always been close, and she was motivated to emulate his interests. Besides *StarCraft,* she and her brother shared an interest in console games, *Yu-Gi-Oh!*, and *Tiberian Sun.* And like some other gamers, Mona started by playing games casually, for example, doing comp stomp (beating computer opponents) and playing for fun. Later, she found videos of professional gaming events on the openly networked internet and fell in love with professional competitions.

Mona elaborated on how difficult it can be for young women to discover their own interest in things that are stereotypically male:

> There's always that issue of access. You don't have girls saying, "Oh, video games, I should play them because they're cool." What I mean by that is that a lot of girls, when they're brought up, they basically do things that their peers are interested in or that their parents give them access to. Because no one tells me that, I'm not going to say, "Hi mom, get me an N64." That's what my brother did because he was like, "Oh, all my guy friends are getting N64s. Mom, get me an N64." Otherwise, girls are only exposed to things like shopping. Your peers are really interested in shopping. Your peers are really interested in books and "hanging out." It's very different, and because of the different exposure that you are given, I feel like it's more difficult to learn how to read a game or learn how to play a game.

Mona suggests that young women ask for things that their peers and parents think are culturally appropriate. If her brother had not asked for video games, she would probably not have had the opportunity to play them.

Having access to video games at home is not the only influencing factor in Mona's development of a geeky interest. She also met like-minded geeky peers in the International Baccalaureate (IB) program at her high school. IB programs expose students to mathematics, science, and critical thinking, which may explain why Mona found many other geeky kids to hang out with. "A lot of us were nerds," she said. There, she met three other female friends with similar backgrounds—they had geeky siblings and were interested in *StarCraft*. They became best friends. Playing competitively online for the first time is a nerve-racking experience for all *StarCraft* players. Mona and her friends supported each other, socially and emotionally, by cheering each other on until they became more confident. At school, they beat the *StarCraft* boys in their class.

Mona speculated that had she not had geeky siblings and peers in her early life, she would have found it difficult to pick up video gaming in college. She provided us with an example by describing expert keyboard manipulation. "What is WASD? You move using those controls in a game. If you only use your computer to check your email, it's incredibly difficult for females to get into the gaming scene." Mona told us that many college women she had met faced similar difficulties. Gaming skills are more complex than simply controlling your mouse to click on icons. Avid gamers develop fine keyboarding skills, such as clicking on the correct keys without even looking at the keyboard, through their frequent usages of common game controls such as WASD. These gamers can pick up new games and become good at them much more easily than others can.

At Princeton University, Mona remained deeply interested in *StarCraft* and looked for like-minded students to form a *StarCraft II* club. She describes how she first recruited participants, joking that a shared geeky Asian identity helped prime the pump. "If I saw an Asian guy who kind of looked Korean, who looked like he might know what *StarCraft* was, I would ask and be like, 'Hey, we should start a *StarCraft* team.' And so I met a lot of people through that process."

After she found a handful of students at Princeton who were interested in *StarCraft II*, the group began organizing matches with other schools:

> We were thinking, "Hey, in two years, if we get 20 schools we will be happy." What happened was, the Princeton students—I started trying to meet the Princeton team—and someone from MIT who was my friend, he said, "Hey, we play StarCraft here, let's have a show match." We thought it was great fun so we made a hype video about it and we broadcast it.
>
> After that, people started emailing us. We did most of this through Team Liquid [a popular *StarCraft* community site]. People were like, "Hey, we want to play too." At first, we were just going to do show matches every week, and I would try to organize them. But eventually we got so many sign-ups that we got 26 people. . . . Then we went up to 144, and now we're at 250.

Through a collaborative effort between Mona and her friends, *Collegiate Starleague* has become an overwhelming success, built on the principles of peer support and shared interests. These college students use their social networks of similar-aged peers to build a league in which players share an interest in *StarCraft II* competition and learning and are identified by the college they are attending. In 2013, participating colleges included the champion University of California, Berkeley; University of California, San Diego; and University of Washington.

2

Affinity

Bonding through Shared Cultures and Practices

Lead Authors: Rachel Cody Pfister and Crystle Martin

Introduction

Maria, a 17-year-old Asian college student from the Philippines, was interviewed as part of Martin's study of online fans of professional wrestling (see the end of chapter 1 for the *Wrestling Boards* case study).[1] She was first introduced to World Wrestling Entertainment (WWE) when her father brought home some wrestling trading cards, and she started to watch WWE when she was a freshman in high school. Her brother would watch with her, but her friends at school teased her and called her a tomboy when she shared her interest in WWE. The online world became a haven for her to connect with peers who shared her interest, and she became an active participant in discussion forums for the WWE fandom. She is particularly active on a role-playing board on the *Wrestling Boards*, where fans write collaborative fanfiction together, creating and taking on the roles of different wrestlers. Through her participation in the *Wrestling Boards*, Maria developed both an interest and skill in writing.

Online affinity networks such as the *Wrestling Boards* are collectives that have shared interests, practices, and marked roles in the community that define levels of responsibility and expertise. These groups are not necessarily limited, however, to the tight ties that one might associate with a "community," though all of them do include participants who have these kinds of personal relationships. Because of their reliance on open peer-to-peer networks, online affinity networks can include large numbers of lurkers, observers, and transient participants, whether they are sporadic readers or readers with casual interests who might browse a forum after a Google search. Indeed, these more casual participants make up the majority of an affinity network (Gee 2017). Even while allowing for lurkers and casual audience members, these online affinity networks are sustained through interpersonal relationships, shared activities, and a sense of cultural affinity. These characteristics distinguish online affinity networks from more traditional media audiences or from a diffuse interest or scene. For example, the *StarCraft* gaming scene is very broad and diffuse, and it includes a constellation of online affinity networks centered on activities such as game modding, or competitive league-based play where some people develop close working relationships with one another. Conversely, an online affinity network is broader than what one might associate with a specific activity or program, such as a summer *StarCraft* program, or a single gaming event, at which participants might gather for a specific period but then disband without forming sustaining practices and relationships.

We describe the groups we have studied as "online affinity networks" to distinguish them from long-standing affinity groups and networks that have predated the online world. We call them "online" affinity networks as a shorthand to distinguish them from affinity networks that are primarily grounded in place-based activities and organizations, and we are not implying that they are not "real," tied to face-to-face interactions, or embedded in physical infrastructures. This chapter delves into the infrastructure, culture, and practices that hold online affinity networks together.

Infrastructure and Space

Ever since its early days, the internet has been an avenue for people to connect with others with shared interests and identities, varying from fandoms, political discourse, and gaming to ethnic, religious, or LGBTQ identities. Howard Rheingold described the unique bonding among participants in early online forums such as the Whole Earth 'Lectronic Link (the WELL) in his book *The Virtual Community* (2000), and many other researchers followed in his footsteps by studying, for example, virtual worlds (Boellstorff 2008; Kendall 2002; Turkle 2005), online groups of gamers (Nardi 2010; Steinkuehler 2008; Taylor 2009), fans (Baym 2000; Bury 2005; Jenkins 2008), and bloggers (Russell and Echchaibi 2009). Eventually, internet platforms such as MySpace and Facebook became mainstream, mirroring the everyday networks that we navigate in school, community, and workplace (boyd 2014). At the same time, niche and interest-centered online communities also continued to proliferate and now encompass almost every imaginable affinity and pursuit. The internet has provided a new infrastructure for people to communicate and organize around interests and affinity with ease and in a more pervasive way. For children and youth who have limited mobility and access to face-to-face affinity groups, the impact of online affinity networks is particularly profound.

In online affinity networks, young people are pursuing what, in our earlier Digital Youth research (Ito et al. 2010), we described as "interest-driven" learning and participation—where they are going online to find information, communities, and learning resources that support specialized interests and affiliations that may not be available in their local communities. In our earlier study, LiveJournal was a gathering spot for these kinds of interactions, which later moved to platforms such as Tumblr or Twitter. We contrasted this with "friendship-driven" forms of online communication through MySpace and instant messaging (IM) and eventually through text messages, Facebook, and Instagram. Teens might discuss romantic relationships and negotiate school-based popularity on Snapchat and Facebook, while they geek out on games, anime, or music on Tumblr and Twitter. While some online affinity networks do use platforms such as Facebook and Instagram, they more typically rely on sites and platforms that allow for more specialized forms of content creation, sharing, and reputation building. Young people describe how they will segment their online identities between the friendship-driven and interest-driven platforms. Often, they will have little overlap between their social networks on Facebook or Instagram and their online affinity networks.

Online affinity networks share some characteristics with long-standing hobby and sports networks, but they are not characterized by the organizational contexts, infrastructures, and face-to-face relations that we associate with these place-based groups. In their analysis of online social networks, Rainie and Wellman (2012) describe how online access is tied to a growing and flexible palette of choices for affiliation and a resulting shift away from affinities grounded in local places and organizations. We see youth online affinity networks as part of this broader trend toward affiliation defined by affinity rather than by geography or organizational membership. While Rainie and Wellman describe this as "networked individualism," our cases indicate a shift toward intentional and tailored group membership rather than individuation. The young people we spoke to stress how online networks enabled them to find a social context for what was previously a solitary interest. We see continuity between place-based affinity networks and online affinity networks in that both support learning and participation that is centered on the pursuit of interests. What differentiates online affinity networks from the hobby and sports groups in a young person's local community is that the infrastructure centers on online space and infrastructure, rather than on brick-and-mortar organizations and settings. Although most hobby and interest groups now have some mix of online and place-based presence, online affinity networks are distinguished in their primary reliance on online infrastructure. We have identified three common features that characterize online affinity networks, which we elaborate on in this section:

1. The network is *specialized*. It is centered on a specific affinity or interest, rather than being layered with other forms of affiliation. Organizations such as schools and workplaces can support affiliation based on specialized interests, but other affiliations and agendas come into play. In schools, teens negotiate romantic and peer relationships and academic competition, as well as pursuing specialized interests. By contrast, in online affinity networks their status centers on knowledge, expertise, and contribution to the interest area.

2. Involvement is *intentional*. It is a voluntary "chosen" affiliation, and not part of a formal professional, school, or governmental affiliation. While some online affinity networks may have formal markers of membership and leadership, contributions and involvement are driven by personal interest and choice. Participants move more fluidly in and out of engagement than in more formal organizations that directly determine young people's academic and economic success.

3. Content sharing and communication take place on *openly networked* online platforms. At least some dimension of every online affinity network is discoverable on the "open" internet, without the gatekeeping of a financial transaction or formal institutional membership. Further, online affinity networks make use of digitally networked infrastructures that allow for broader visibility and access than place-based forms of communication.

Relationships in online affinity networks are by definition specialized in that they are centered on a particular identity or interest. They differ from the more multilayered relationships that young people navigate at home, in school, and in local activities. They are likely to encounter their families and school friends in multiple settings that can vary from social hanging out to more specialized kinds of pursuits such as athletics. By contrast, online affinity networks are structured around particular niche pursuits, whether that is modding in *StarCraft* or knitting items related to *Harry Potter*. Further, the way people achieve status and recognition in online affinity networks is highly targeted to engagement in a specific area of interest, rather than to other factors such as "real-world" popularity and attractiveness or the ability to garner attention online in a generic way. In other words, online affinity networks are unique in being optimized around a particular affinity and related pursuits. The groups we have studied are particularly distinctive in valuing niche forms of expertise. *Harry Potter* fans gain status through the knowledge of the extensive lore and trivia around the series, and *StarCraft* players win recognition by working their way up the competitive rankings of a challenging game. The workings of status and reputation systems in online affinity networks are the focus of the next chapter.

The other important dimension of these relationships is that they are *intentional*—young people make conscious choices to connect and maintain connection, unlike relationships they are born into or relationships that are sustained as part of a job or at school, or for instrumental reasons. With this intentional quality comes a sense of authenticity as well as ephemerality in that it is easy to disconnect when an interest wanes or other responsibilities crowd out discretionary time. Online affinity networks do not have the layered and resilient characteristics of relationships embedded in schools and other community institutions, but in exchange, they are also free from the status hierarchies that characterize these social networks for teens. Young people describe how they go online to play games and connect with fandoms without having to worry about issues of status, popularity, and the heterosexual marketplace that are omnipresent in their face-to-face networks. For those who might feel stigmatized by displaying their creative, fannish, or nerdy interests to their friends at school, online affinity networks represent an opportunity to geek out with people who share their passions and

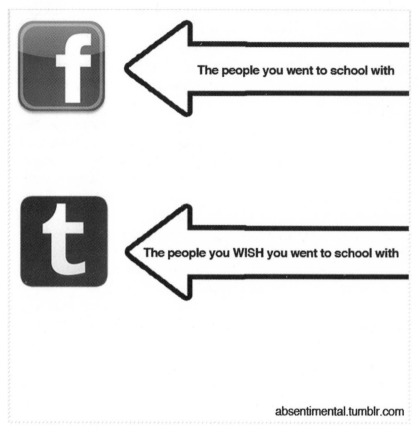

Figure 2.1. A meme circulated on Tumblr (absentimental.tumblr.com).

support their learning (see, for example, figure 2.1). Status and reputation in online affinity networks can be just as exclusionary and unforgiving as in the high school cafeteria, but they are centered on a chosen set of affiliations and are easier to escape.

With the intentional and targeted nature of online affinity networks comes certain risks. Although we focus on groups with positive social values, other groups can reinforce problematic perspectives and pursuits. What we see as positive "geeking out" can pivot to a negative form of extremism, with peers reinforcing niche views without the checks and balances that come from family, local community, and those with different interests and affinities. We recognize these risks, and we focus on the features of prosocial and learning-oriented online affinity networks in an effort to highlight and advocate for positive community values online. We believe that this approach complements other studies that have looked at more controversial forms of "geeking out" online (Boero and Pascoe 2012; G. Coleman 2014; Massanari 2017; Yeshua-Katz and Martins 2013).

In addition to supporting specialized and intentional affiliation, another common feature of online affinity networks is that they rely on *openly networked* infrastructures for communication and content sharing. This characteristic of online affinity networks is what differentiates them from more traditional place-based affinity networks, which generally have much higher barriers to access. Young people of all skill levels are publishing, circulating, and commenting on each other's performances and creations in a "networked public" (Varnelis 2012). When dancers post their videos on YouTube, fanfiction writers publish on the online platform Wattpad, or gamers screencast their competitive play, the creative production of online affinity networks becomes visible and searchable to broad audiences. While young people are also engaging in private communication and face-to-face encounters with peers they meet through their online affinity networks, the circulation of content and communication on open and public networks is a distinguishing characteristic of online affinity networks.

Openly sharing through peer-to-peer networks is fundamental to the platforms that support online affinity networks. Spaff serves as the community manager of *Sackboy Planet,* a player-created online design community (the case study appears at the end of chapter 3). He described the value of level sharing for *LittleBigPlanet 2* players and the collective: "You can create your own levels, your own games, and then people can play them, but they can't play them if you can't share them. So the community really is filled with people who are spending hours and hours and hours building their own levels, their own games, then they publish them onto the Internet. . . . We have just over 6 million levels and games up there now . . . other people can find those levels and play them, rate them, be inspired by them, create their own things." *LittleBigPlanet 2* players can access a wide range of levels from which they may be inspired to poach, remix, sample, or build on. In turn, creators are also able to receive feedback through sharing, improving their own craft.

For young people first dipping into an area of interest, online affinity networks give them an opportunity to search, lurk, and become familiar with a scene without risk or exposure. As they get more involved in the online affinity network, they might comment or share some of their own work online and get their first taste of connecting with an audience and getting feedback. In turn, their continued sharing in an open network becomes a beacon for new seekers. Openly networked infrastructures supported these dynamics for Katie, a 15-year-old white teen from Australia. Discovering fanfiction online through the Wattpad app was her first step to becoming an author (see the 1D on Wattpad case study at the end of this chapter). By reading the work of other teen One Direction fans, she found "people who have been writing their own stories and they were people just like me." Madeleine, a 15-year-old white teen from Canada, was nervous about sharing her work on Wattpad, fearing people would "judge me and post hate comments." Instead, through sharing her work, Madeleine was able to make "a bunch of friends and people asked me to co-write with them." Her identity as an author was affirmed, and she felt confident in then sharing her works with a school friend. Madeleine also found inspiration when reading the works that others had created, finding new ideas but also learning from the ways that other authors created stories.

Online affinity networks tend to follow the "Pareto principle," in which 20 percent of participants contribute 80 percent of the network's outcomes, with the top 1 percent contributing the most (Gee 2017). Our research has focused on the active participants, with a bias toward the 1 percent, among whom we are most likely to find connected learners. Although the more visible participants carry most of the load for organizing and creating content, casual participants and lurkers also engage in important forms of participation that sustain the reach, visibility, and influence of the network. Sustaining the whole range of participation and contribution in online affinity networks is a constant struggle for community organizers, given the intentional and voluntary nature of affiliation. Later in this chapter we describe some of the challenges that community organizers face in maintaining robust participation. Other studies of youth engagement with digital media indicate that, unlike those in our study, most are not inclined to take an active role in online affinity networks (Ito et al. 2010; Livingstone and Sefton-Green 2016).

In particular, young people growing up in less tech-savvy families are much less likely to actively contribute to online affinity networks (Martin, forthcoming). Our study seeks to identify the characteristics of young people who counter this trend so that we can design programs that guide a wider range of young people to these opportunities.

As more and more young people go online, smartphones spread, and online affinity networks proliferate, we can expect that they will become more central to how young people socialize, learn, and pursue interests. In our earlier Digital Youth study (Ito et al. 2010), based on fieldwork in 2006–2007, teens described a stigma associated with meeting new friends online—the pull of local relationships and the status and social capital derived from local place-based friendships exerted a much stronger influence on their online participation than online affinity networks. This dynamic may be changing, however. Our current study focused on active participants in online affinity networks, so it is not surprising that they were comfortable with making online friends through affinity groups. More recent survey research indicates that online friendships have become commonplace, so norms may be shifting. The majority of U.S. teens now say they have met a new friend online (Lenhart et al. 2015). The role of online affinity networks likely is growing in young people's lives.

Shared Culture and Knowledge

At the heart of any affinity network is a set of shared interests, identities, culture, and values that bind participants together. While online affinity networks exist for every imaginable interest area, our cases suggest they may be particularly active and robust for groups that are specialized, lack a critical mass in local communities, and hold to high standards of knowledge and expertise. In other words, people tend to congregate in online affinity networks when they want to geek out with others who are fellow enthusiasts, and when they lack these relationships in their offline lives. They often feel a particularly profound sense of belonging to these groups because of this shared niche culture and identity.

For example, a shared interest in both fiber crafting and *Harry Potter* is a niche combination that lacks a critical mass in most local communities but is a magnet for more than 1,000 participants to connect on

Ravelry (see the *Hogwarts at Ravelry* case study at the end of chapter 4). "We all belong here," said Amazon, a white 28-year-old based in Cleveland and a member of *Hogwarts at Ravelry*. Her description of why she loves *Hogwarts at Ravelry* captures how a shared passion for a niche interest binds members of an online affinity network. "The camaraderie and instant friendship, especially in your own house, though inter-house love is also prevalent. I can talk to someone I've never met before and because of the history inherent at Hogwarts, we've passed each other in the halls [of our virtual school] a thousand times. We go to the same charms class. We know the same lingo, share the same inside jokes."

Amazon describes the unique pleasure of sharing cultural context and insider references with others with shared tastes, passions, and expertise. These shared cultural elements are important to creating, enriching, and sustaining relationships (Fine 1979). Rich content worlds such as the *Harry Potter* series offer a trove of specialized knowledge that provides ample fodder for geeking out and social organizing by engaged fan communities (Jenkins 2012).

Anime fandom exhibits a similar dynamic. Although anime has become a popular "meganiche" (Shirky 2006) outside of Japan, the breadth of content and fan activity means that the online world supports a wide range of highly specialized affinity networks within the fandom. The anime music video (AMV) scene is one such niche, a network that centers on the specific practices of video remix within the broader anime fandom (see the Animemusicvideos.org case study at the end of chapter 3). Gepetto,[2] an 18-year-old from Brazil who had been an anime fan for some time, describes the moment when he first discovered AMVs. He was shocked to realize that the AMV was created by "a fan just like me." As he recounts this memory, he continues, "Actually, my heart is racing right now just remembering. Of course, I'm a weird person but it's still racing." After discovering AMVs, Gepetto went on to become an active participant in animemusicvideos.org, a center of gravity for the AMV community. "I love the forums, I love the chats, I love answering questions and having mine answered in turn. I could spend 24 hours straight discussing AMVs without so much as a coffee break." His ongoing interest and engagement are fueled by the shared referents and connoisseurship of anime, as well as the deep technical expertise around video remixing that is discussed in the forums.

A pursuit of expertise also fuels networks built around competitive esports such as *StarCraft II*. *StarCraft II* represents a highly tuned arena for players and fans to compete and strive for excellence (see the end of chapter 1 for the case study). In these competitive affinity networks, young people will connect online or in tournaments outside their local communities to pursue an ongoing challenge. Often their affinity network will include a mix of local peers as well as online networks that allow them to specialize and level up. Mona Zhang,[3] a 22-year-old Asian college student from New Jersey, vividly recalled how relationships forged through *StarCraft II* motivated her to do her best in game matches; she remembered "getting butterflies in my stomach because I have to play for my team and I don't want to let them down." Victor, a 16-year-old high school junior from California, recalled how watching a *StarCraft II* tournament and feeling a part of a community that shared his passion provided the rush and drive to pursue his interest in *StarCraft II*. Remembering the tournament, he noted, "I can't even emphasize how addicted that made me to *StarCraft* as a game. I saw that and I was like, this is it. This is the game that I'm going to play. This is the community that I want to be a part of and this is what I want to do for a really long time."

Another pull that draws young people to connect online is if an interest is stigmatized. Online affinity networks provide an attractive safe haven, even when young people might have local friends who share the interests. Some among the One Direction fanfiction writers and members of the *Wrestling Boards* we spoke to felt they needed to hide their interests from their local communities. Boyband fandom is generally not culturally valued, particularly among adults, and many fans of One Direction did not share their interests with teachers and parents. Katie, the 15-year-old Australian we met earlier in this chapter, said that although she was a prolific writer, she did not feel comfortable telling her teachers about her fanfiction because they "wouldn't get it plus they would ask questions." Katie even felt wary sharing her interests in some online spaces, as she had experienced hostility toward 1D fangirling on a social media site. As she explained, "There are people on there that we don't so much want to see us fangirling over one direction because they will judge so we tend to stick to websites where we know we are in good company."

Stigma among their peers was also a concern for many WWE fans, even though many came into the interest through their families. Jonathan, a white 16-year-old from the United Kingdom and a participant on the *Wrestling Boards* (the case study appears at the end of chapter 1), said that wrestling was viewed negatively in his area, and that "no one that I know likes WWE as they see it as being 'childish' or 'immature.'" WacoKid, a white and Native American male in his 30s from Texas, said that although conversations in his local community would sometimes reveal people's wrestling interests, generally they kept the interest to themselves and did not openly discuss or participate in the fandom: "For the most part, WWE fans (or any pro wrestling fans) around here seem to be in the closet." For these fans, their wrestling interests were not just unsupported by their local communities; they were something to be hidden.

For participants in One Direction fanfiction and the *Wrestling Boards* forums, the online affinity networks provided a space where they could identify with their peers as fans, makers, artists, and writers. For the Noob, a white 17-year-old from the United Kingdom, participating in the *Wrestling Boards* helped make a shift in his identity. He describes how he used to wonder "'do people feel I am stupid for liking WWE etc' but when I found out about the *Wrestling Boards,* knowing there were loads of people my age, it boosted my confidence in liking WWE." Through the *Wrestling Boards,* he found validation and support among peers. Mike, an 18-year-old white male from Michigan, found that having a space where his interests were recognized "has allowed me to express myself about a lot of things or topics that I can't really talk to people about around where I live due to lack of interest."

While online affinity networks generally focus on a particular interest, participants will still bring in different interests and cultural referents and engage in "off-topic" discussion. Through these other interests, participants can contribute varied skills and experiences to the online affinity network and open up new opportunities for collaboration or relationship building. Farooq, an 18-year-old African American male from San Diego, mixed his love of the *My Little Pony* television series with his interest in professional wrestling, making *My Little Pony* and WWE mashups in his online signature images. In *Hogwarts at Ravelry,* participants often discussed other popular series such as *Doctor Who* or *Supernatural.* In one *Hogwarts at Ravelry* class, a crocheted Dalek from the *Doctor Who* series was submitted as an example of something Harry Potter could use against the Dursleys. The image that accompanied the

Figure 2.2. A Dalek versus *My Little Pony* toys.
Photo by Rachel Cody Pfister.

submission included the Dalek aiming at *My Little Pony* toys, a combination of two popular series (see figure 2.2) creatively linked to the main interests of *Hogwarts at Ravelry*.

Anime fans will play and debate video games together, and *StarCraft* players might jump to a game of *Hearthstone* or *Pokémon* to blow off steam. The communities we studied had threads and boards that participants could use to discuss other interests, but they are clearly marked as "off topic." As long as the core affinity that ties the network together remains robust, groups thrive on points of intersection with other subcultures and cultural referents.

Factors that draw young people to online spaces to pursue their interests are diverse. For some, it is to find a safe space for a stigmatized interest. For others, it is because of an attraction to a narrow niche, leveling up, or technical specialization that is accessible only online. In all cases, however, high-functioning online affinity networks are characterized by a strong shared culture and set of values that are the magnet for affiliation. In addition, a set of shared practices provides a focus of activity and engagement.

Shared Practices

Activity in online affinity networks is fueled by shared practices that give focus and direction to participation in the network. Activities that support connected learning center on organized production, collaboration, and competition that create a sense of shared purpose. These learning-oriented online affinity networks are examples of what Henry Jenkins has called "participatory culture"—"a culture with relatively low barriers to artistic expression and civic engagement, strong support for creating and sharing one's creations, and some type of informal mentorship whereby what is known by the most experienced is passed along to novices" (Jenkins et al. 2009:xi). In these online affinity networks, participants are not simply consuming media but are actively involved in creation, circulation, curation, and commentary. We describe three forms of shared practices that we found to be at the heart of online affinity networks that support learning, creation, and expertise: collaborative production, competitions, and community organizing.

Collaborative Production

Collaborative production offers members opportunities to engage in meaningful and hands-on learning in which they blend skills, envision new creations, and build affinity as they work toward the shared purpose of the community (Ito 2012b; Ito et al. 2013; Moran and John-Steiner 2004; Searle 2004). The Leveling Up cases highlight the diverse kinds of products that can be supported through collaborative production. In the *Wrestling Boards* and *Hogwarts at Ravelry*, for example, collaborative production happens as a group-level collective endeavor to build fantasy worlds around shared interests. Collaborative production in the One Direction fanfiction, Bollywood dance, and *Sackboy Planet* affinity networks results in a more tangible product, such as stories, dance choreographies, and game levels. These types of collaborative production foster the blending of specialized knowledge toward collective goals.

In the *Wrestling Boards* and *Hogwarts at Ravelry*, participants collaboratively craft fantasy worlds through which members can pursue their

Figure 2.3. A screen shot of a video of Rhashan performing a wrestling promo for his fantasy wrestling character.

Image courtesy of Rhashan.

shared interests. In the *Wrestling Boards*, members role-play as wrestlers, write background stories for their characters, and carry out wrestling matches with other members through the coordinated exchange of creative writing and role-play (as seen in figure 2.3). *Hogwarts at Ravelry* members (see the case study at the end of chapter 4) similarly use role-playing and fiber crafting to build a fantasy world that parallels the Hogwarts school of the *Harry Potter* series. For example, in a discussion about moving a conversation to a different message board thread, KnittingPrincipal,[4] a 43-year-old white woman from Idaho and the leader of *Hogwarts at Ravelry*, switched to role-play and began "*waving wand frantically . . . shouting* WHOOSH*!!!*" In other small moments, members "dropped their suitcases" in the discussion threads for their houses as new school years began and sometimes would "trip over broomsticks" lying around in classes. These small moments of role-play continually reinforce the fantasy world of the group. Images of crafted items are also abundant and help create a visual representation of the fantasy world; Hagrid's pumpkin patch was re-created through knit pumpkin toys (see figure 2.4) and crocheted pot holders, and members filled the Great Hall's tables with images of crocheted food items at

Figure 2.4. *Hogwarts at Ravelry* members post images of pumpkin-themed crafted items to re-create Hagrid's pumpkin patch.

Photo by Rachel Cody Pfister.

Thanksgiving. The small moments of role-playing—attaching graphics to posts, or writing wrestler backgrounds—help signal identity and belonging to the affinity network and provide a collective frame to engage other members.

The Bollywood dance case study (at the end of this chapter) is of an online affinity network centered on production and competition in dance performance. Members of university dance teams combine specialized skills and work together to craft a Bollywood dance performance. Akash, a college student from California, used his engineering skills to build props, his musical interests to research and develop hip-hop–inspired choreography, and his filmography interests to create introductory videos for his team's competitions. Neesha, a college student from Palo Alto, learned to use GarageBand to create sound mixes for her team. Other roles included costume designing, fundraising, and the creation of stories for performances.

The One Direction fan community on the Wattpad online publishing platform centers on the production of fanfiction and media related to One Direction. Most fanfiction benefits from some type of collective feedback or suggestions, and some authors also create "collab-accounts" through which multiple authors collaboratively produce a work. It is also common for members to work collaboratively on a project through a "blending of skills" (Moran and John-Steiner 2004:11). For example, one person might write a fanfiction story while another person creates the book cover graphics to accompany the story. Additionally, some members work together to collaboratively produce .gifs, or short looping digital images, around their One Direction interests. Similarly, *Nerdfighters* use collab channels on YouTube to help overcome some of the challenges of online production (see the case study at the end of chapter 4). Creative production is a high-effort endeavor. Producing a video involves multiple stages of planning, scripting, filming, editing, posting, and tagging. By joining forces, young Nerdfighters lower the bar to entry to posting videos to YouTube and to the expectation of maintaining constantly updated content.

The *Sackboy Planet* affinity network also offers an example of how collaborative production involves the combining and blending of specialized knowledge and skills (see the end of chapter 3 for the case study). The shared purpose of this affinity network is the construction of *LittleBigPlanet 2* game levels. *Sackboy Planet* members devote much of their creative energy to level design, *LittleBigPlanet 2*'s most innovative feature. Participants can not only play the main side-scrolling video game in Story mode, but they can also use Create mode to produce unique game levels that can be shared with others. Among the many features of Create mode is an option for players to "co-create," or produce level designs together with other players. Multiple players "hang out" in the same level-creation sandbox, and each has the ability to tinker and develop the level. On *Sackboy Planet*, a *LittleBigPlanet 2* companion community, players find others with whom to co-create levels.

Many complex skills go into level creation, including game design, programming, art, story development, and scripting. Players use the level-design forum of *Sackboy Planet* to find others with whom to create levels; they post a thread asking others with specific skill sets to join forces and create a level. In this way, the players function like game-development teams, each contributing his or her area of expertise to produce a more expert level. Kengo Kurimoto,[5] a level-design lead at Media Molecule, pointed out that in the game-development industry, "there's a music guy and a graphics guy and an artificial intelligence guy, and all these different roles, and I think that's kind of happened a little bit in *LittleBigPlanet* where often teams get together and somebody does the music score and somebody else does the game play and somebody else does the costumes and that kind of thing. It's pretty neat."

Kurimoto said that "what really is exciting about working with other creative people is the surprises." Co-creating can expose players to ideas and approaches they might not have come up with on their own. Kurimoto goes on to say of collaboration that "ultimately, it's definitely the best way to do things." Co-creation presents opportunities for designers to combine their specific design skills and ideas in a way that can produce a collaborative and creative synergy. Ninjadude, a white 19-year-old from the United States, pointed out that collectively sharing insights and new ideas was an important part of level creation. When players asked him for help, he went "in and helped them with specific things," and he would "take a look at it and try to figure it out."

Sackboy Planet demonstrates how collaborative production can play a powerful role in supporting shared purpose through building connections and combining skills. Players acquire and advance their skills through meaningful activities, embodying their learning as they build, tinker, and troubleshoot levels. The complex and diverse skills required to build levels encourage players to form connections with others and combine their specialized knowledge, gain creative insights, and produce a more masterful level than any one player could build. This collaborative production advances individual learning, but it also advances the collective shared purpose through building affinity and producing more creative and more expert levels.

Contests and Challenges

Contests and challenges are another category of collective practice that can motivate and structure engagement in online affinity networks that are oriented to developing skills and expertise, and they are particularly salient in affinity networks centered on competitive games such as *StarCraft II* (see the end of chapter 1 for the case study). The *Star-Craft II* online platform matches players based on past performance on "the ladder," providing continuous challenge, transparent ranking, and the potential for leveling up. In addition to this everyday play and practice, the *StarCraft II* community organizes a host of tournaments for different levels of players, including the pro leagues, the after-hours gaming league for working professionals, the *Collegiate Starleague*, and the *High School Starleague*. Another popular informal social format is "BarCraft," in which players commandeer sports bars for an after-work competition. Social viewing of this kind is an important vehicle for players and fans to develop a more sophisticated understanding of sports. Games such as *StarCraft* have earned the moniker "esports" because of similarities with traditional sports; esports have professional players, spectators and fans, and high-stakes competitions. Further, because players can compete at any time of day and night with comparatively little physical exhaustion, the performance and practice demands of esports are in some ways more relentless than those of traditional athletics.

Competition is a source of creative inspiration in *Over the Ropes*, the fantasy wrestling federation of the *Wrestling Boards* (see the end of chapter 1 for the case study). Writers co-construct fantasy wrestling matches using role-play and narratives. At the beginning of a season, players describe their character's background, physical characteristics, wrestling style, moves, and appearance. The community selects a booker, who manages the fantasy wrestling federation and decides which players will participate. Selected players spend the first part of the week role-playing dialogue with their opponents and co-constructing a story line. Rubin, for example, role-played as his wrestler Trent Dixon and taunted his opponent, "Do whatever the hell you want, chuck in another 7 guys for all I care, I'll just dismantle them in exactly the way I plan to do to Exterminator." The booker awards points for quality, authenticity, and quantity. At the end of the week, the exchanges, or "feuds," between the two wrestlers are compiled into a narrative, with the winner determined by the number of points given by the booker. Better collaboration results in a better story line and more points. The point system rewards collaborative competitions and group participation, and motivates members to accumulate more wrestling knowledge and improve their writing abilities.

Gryffindor 56,150   Ravenclaw 49,397   Slytherin 44,280   Hufflepuff 44,932

Figure 2.5. Members of *Hogwarts at Ravelry* participate in classes and challenges to earn house points in hopes of winning the House Cup.
Image courtesy of KnittingPrincipal.

Similarly, a competitive narrative powers the fantasy world of *Hogwarts at Ravelry* (see the end of chapter 4 for the case study). The penultimate competition is the House Cup, for which the different houses—or subcommunities of the group—compete (see figure 2.5). Members participate in classes and challenges that push them to learn more about their *Harry Potter* interests, advance their crafting skills, and embody this learning through producing crafted items. The staff of *Hogwarts at Ravelry* grade members' submissions to these classes and challenges, and those points go toward the members' houses in the House Cup competition. This competition provides motivation for members to participate, learn, and produce written essays or crafted items. Professor Briana,[6] a 25-year-old white woman and an active community member from Utah, asked students to complete a star chart, wherein they would discover that major *Harry Potter* characters were named after stars and constellations. One herbology class assignment asked Mary, a 21-year-old white woman from Canada, to learn more about the magical herb gillyweed and to craft an item with "bobbles" to represent the gillyweed. Through this assignment, Mary drew on her knowledge of the fourth *Harry Potter* book and looked to a knitting book, and then her mother, to learn the bobble stitch.

The challenges of *Hogwarts at Ravelry* also provide an accessible way for novices to enter the group and engage with their housemates. The House Unity projects, for example, are intrahouse collaborative challenges that help build affinity within a house while also socializing new members to the group's practices. In the House Unity projects, house members choose a theme and craft items related to that theme, and then all post images of their crafted items on the same day in a chosen location. For example, Hufflepuff bombarded the headmistress's office with breakfast items in one House Unity project, and Ravenclaw launched fireworks in the Great Hall using the same narrative attached to the various crafted items: "Sputtering sparks shoot up towards the ceiling as a firework is let off in the Great Hall."

In *Sackboy Planet* (see the case study at the end of chapter 3), contests and challenges were not a central practice, but they offered a means through which to build affinity outside of the primary production practices. Although there were official *LittleBigPlanet 2* challenges that provided an important means to gaining audiences and status (see chapter 3, "Status: Developing Social and Cultural Capital"), there were also smaller unofficial challenges that the players themselves organized. In these contests, a player could use knowledge and experience gained in *LittleBigPlanet 2* to create a contest that would appeal to other players. For example, Jaron, a 27-year-old white male from the United States, was "helping plan and execute the very first LBP Hunger Games competition." Ninjadude, introduced above, organized a "caption contest," in which the organizer would give a "blank scene that would be kind of funny and everyone would enter and put their caption on. What are the sack people in this thing thinking or saying?" This contest provided a type of participation in the *LittleBigPlanet 2* affinity network very different from the usual game playing and level creation while still drawing on the shared interests of the players.

In the Bollywood dance scene (see the case study at the end of this chapter), competitions are a growing force in structuring and motivating participation. They include both regional and national events, with Bollywood America as the penultimate competition. Thousands of dancers organize through Facebook and more specialized channels such as desidanceteams.com. Preparing for a competition is a major endeavor that includes not only choreographing and practicing dance, but fundraising, creating videos, and making props and costumes. This pride and excitement around creative competitions are also evident in Wattpad, where a range of official and community-sponsored challenges are an ongoing focus of attention for young writers. In particular, the annual Watty Awards are a centerpiece of the competitive landscape of

Wattpad. The AMV world also organizes around competitions. Most major anime conventions feature an AMV screening and competition, which is one of the most well-attended events. Xstylus[7], a 28-year-old white male, describes the moment when his video was recognized as a winner at a major convention: "The massive auditorium gave me a standing ovation. The only people who could ever come close to experiencing such a feeling are Hollywood directors having won an Academy Award for Best Picture. It was the finest, greatest, most moving moment of my entire existence. Nothing will ever top it. Ever."

Winning competitions is the penultimate form of recognition for video editors, and awards are proudly displayed on their online profiles. Animemusicvideos.org also organizes annual viewers' choice awards in addition to a wide range of "top" lists and rankings that are based on community scoring and reviews of videos.

Community Organizing

Maintaining engagement and shared activities in an online affinity network requires ongoing dedicated work on the part of community organizers. Affinity networks are not static; membership is constantly changing and shifting as new members enter, novices become more advanced, and members leave or become less active. Subgroups can come together to organize a new activity or network. Tensions and conflicts can arise as needs or practices change; the affinity networks and groups must evolve to continue to maintain, adapt, and grow to meet these changing needs (Pfister 2016). *Nerdfighters* are constantly thinking up new mobilizations and collaborations to engage their network, Bollywood dancers organize competitions around the country, and fanfiction writers organize fan clubs and promotions. *Hogwarts at Ravelry* members create new challenges each year and offer opportunities for members to connect with other Ravelry groups or local communities. All of the affinity networks we examined rely to a significant degree on volunteer community organizing to kick-start the community, maintain it, and adapt it through time.

Several of our interviewees in the *StarCraft II* case study (see the end of chapter 1) were founding members of communities within the broader affinity network. One of our interviewees, Duran Parsi,[8] a college student in his mid-20s from California, organized the first national league, known as *War of the States*, in 2005. He went on to engage in other community-building efforts such as the *North American Star League* and the *Collegiate Starleague*. After arriving at Princeton, Mona Zhang, the 22-year-old college student introduced earlier in this chapter, started a *StarCraft II* club, and after a time she began organizing matches with other universities in the area. Eventually this network blossomed into a national *Collegiate Starleague*. Her position as a founder of the *Collegiate Starleague* has created opportunities for her to work with BarCraft, practice public relations, and manage a national organization. Another one of our interviewees, Alex, a 15-year-old white male high school student from Florida, is a founding member of the *High School Starleague (HSL)*, made up of 131 teams with at least five members each, and which was inspired by the *Collegiate Starleague*. It was similarly kick-started as a grassroots effort by students. While corporate-sponsored and organized tournaments are part of the overall landscape of esports, the bread and butter of the affinity network, whether it is the various leagues or online communities such as *Team Liquid*, are organized and maintained by community members who put in tremendous amounts of time and effort.

The AMV community and its myriad online sites and competitions were also founded and maintained by dedicated groups of volunteers who have contributed tremendous amounts of time and resources. One organizer, whom Ito interviewed, developed the technologies that enabled the first AMV competitions and screenings at the flagship convention, Anime Weekend Atlanta. He describes how he developed the process for organizing submissions, editing the footage, and putting on the show, donating thousands of dollars' worth of equipment to the cause. All of the conventions are run "by fans for fans," and they receive at most a free hotel stay to organize events serving thousands of participants; the AMV competitions are no exception. One veteran convention organizer describes how "when I first saw some amvs, I thought this was amazing, and I want to do something to support this." He goes on to say that he has no artistic talent himself, but he gives to the community by organizing the events. Animemusicvideos.org was also founded by a fan who developed a custom website that enabled editors to upload, rank, review, and comment on AMVs at a time when no commercial video-sharing sites existed. The site continues to be maintained by volunteer organizers and has weathered many technology changes as well as the mainstreaming of internet video.

Change and adaptation are a constant challenge for community organizing. During Martin's time studying the *Wrestling Boards*, administrators struggled to keep up with moderating, scoring, and offering constructive feedback on the group's numerous shows. Additionally, participation from members was not as high as it should have been, and previous efforts at adding new shows in which members expressed an interest had not succeeded. Amid the strain on the administrators and the waning participation, Sackfist, a 19-year-old male from the United States and the leader of the group, announced the closing of several wrestling shows: "We cannot dedicate the time to write the amount of segments each week . . . at the moment it has a lot of pressure on us because of increased workload of members stepping down [from admin positions]." In response to Sackfist's announcement, members collectively acknowledged the stress that the administrators were under and offered their support of a "reboot" of the fantasy wrestling world.

Sackfist initiated these changes when he announced the closing of several shows. His announcement garnered 32 pages of response, with the majority of the group in support of a reboot. With this reboot, the fantasy wrestling world would start fresh, and the fantasy world's prior history, including wrestling matches and points, would be left in the "old universe." Within the discussion of the reboot, members agreed that the practices should focus on "quality over quantity," as Rhashan, a 19-year-old African American male from New Jersey, put it. Instead of a large number of shows, the focus of the affinity network would be on centralizing participation to a few shows. The structure of matches would remain the same, allowing members to draw from their wrestling experiences and storytelling skills to co-construct matches with other players. The smaller number of shows, however, helped players engage with each other more. The staff could also devote more energy to offering feedback, thereby helping members advance their wrestling interests and storytelling skills.

Pfister also saw organizers of *Hogwarts at Ravelry* struggle to keep participants engaged. In the summer of 2012, group membership had started to decrease. Through discussion, analysis, and sharing of experiences, leaders and veteran members identified a group rule as being the root of the problem. The rule allowed members to submit the same crafted item to multiple challenges or classes, creating pressure to do so as members sought to maximize their points for the House Cup competition. Jen2291,[9] an active participant and 49-year-old white woman from Arizona, pointed to these pressures when she said, "There is a perceived pressure to post [items] everywhere—or you are just leaving points on the table. . . . It takes more time for me to figure out how to connect the same project to all those different prompts as it did to make the darn thing." Participation in the group began to decline as members felt either unable to keep up or guilty for "letting their house down" by not participating more. After the source of the problem was identified, the rules were changed so that each crafted item could be submitted to only one contest or challenge. The leaders implemented these changes with carefully coordinated role-play that tied in the narrative and events of the *Harry Potter* series. The changes were well received by members, with one person cheering, "I ABSOLUTELY LOVE THE CHANGES!" Some members posted how the changes would increase their ability to participate and the quality of the group overall, with Amazon saying, "It will be good to be able to handle the classes again."

Community organizers span a range—from those with official titles and roles to more informal organizing. The core organizing team for the *Sackboy Planet* affinity network is made up of community administrators, but at times other members of the community would take the initiative to assemble offbeat activities. For example, PonyPal, a 17-year-old Latino male from the United States, was bored of the typical level-creation contests that emphasize particular skill sets he was never quite good at. "These were the only kind of contests I saw," he said. "And you'd usually see the same winners of each of the contests." So PonyPal took matters into his own hands and re-created a challenge-based game based on the *Survivor* television series that he used to run during his high school creative writing class. He posted a call for the activity in the *Sackboy Planet* forums, and each season (a period of months) would include 16 challenges within a level he created. Affinity network participants would assemble into teams and join PonyPal's level to attempt to solve the puzzle. "We had stuff where you had to build crazy contraptions live in-game using jet packs and weirdness," he explained. "I'd post up each challenge, and each challenge was a little bit different." PonyPal's *Survivor* competitions drew great interest from the community, particularly because they emphasized other sets of talents not typically rewarded by other competitions—teamwork and rapid-fire problem solving.

Community organizing for online affinity networks is a multifaceted and multitiered process that requires constant innovation, adaptation, and change. Online groups vary in how leadership is structured, their tolerance for off-topic discussion, and how formally norms and community standards are articulated and enforced. Online affinity networks that seek to maintain both a high quality and quantity of discourse and production, such as the ones we studied, face the added challenge of quality control. Organizers need to keep participants focused and engaged in often ambitious projects, goals, and competitions, and they need to regulate what they see as problematic or trollish behaviors. These dynamics are described in more depth in the following chapter. The constants across all online affinity networks with engaged participation are a core group of highly committed volunteer organizers and an active community performing the ongoing labor needed to maintain high levels of participation. No affinity network can rest on its laurels given the constant competition for attention and engagement.

Conclusion

Online affinity networks are a unique genre of social and cultural organization that has emerged with the growth of digital networks. They share many similarities with affinity networks that are rooted in places, such as sports, creative groups, and other community-based organizations. What makes them unique, however, is that they are leveraging open online networks to create specialized niches that often have lower barriers to participation than place-based groups. This means that young people today have the opportunity to connect with peers who share interests that may not have a critical mass in their local communities or in their families, and they have the opportunity to go deeply into these specialties. The distributed and voluntary nature of these networks means, however, that organizers confront an ongoing challenge of designing and adapting shared practices and of maintaining participation. In this chapter, we have described what ties online affinity networks together: their shared infrastructural properties, how they build shared culture around niche identities, and how they organize shared activities. We have focused on the practices of creative production, competition, and community organizing that animate the online affinity networks centered on learning and expertise that are the focus of our study. The following chapter will delve more deeply into the social dynamics, hierarchies, and status systems in these networks to understand how they are internally differentiated.

1D on Wattpad

Ksenia Korobkova

What will happen next?[1] Where should this story go? You click the "Discover" section of the website for inspiration. If Harry Styles, the pop singer and member of One Direction, ended up in an apocalyptic vampire novel, what kind of outfit would he wear? As you answer this question and write the next chapter of your fanfiction novel on the story-sharing app Wattpad, you get yet another comment from a restless fan: "I can't wait until the new chapter comes out!" Dozens of your followers on Wattpad have been asking for the next chapter—eager to find out what happens with the apocalyptic vampire Harry. You post the new chapter. Likes and comments pour in. The next design decision has to be made: What will be on the cover of this story (see examples in figure C.2.1)?

Wattpad (www.wattpad.com) is one of the most popular online platforms for producing and consuming stories. As such, it is part of an array of online tools that transform the ways young people write, read, and share different texts. Originally termed the "story-sharing website," Wattpad is a mobile app, a network of author communities, and a software platform for writing and reading online. Through Wattpad, young people involve themselves in practices of composition, communication, and co-creation as they find new audiences and fellow fans online.

Fans passionate about different content worlds (e.g., books, movies, bands) use Wattpad to further their interest and produce new texts powered by these interests. The platform has become a critical infrastructure that has helped users (more than 25 million worldwide) join and develop affinity networks (Vincent 2014). As a prime example, a group of young female fans called the *Directioners*—or fans of the British boyband One Direction—use the site to exchange information about the band, write fiction stories that are connected to the band, and produce media (book covers, trailers, animated pictures) to showcase their fandom. Most of

Figure C.2.1. Examples of book covers from Wattpad.
Images courtesy of Maya, Abigail, and Emily.

these fanfiction writers, including 26 *Directioners* I interviewed, identify as girls (92 percent), teenagers (14- to 19-year-olds), and "fangirls." I also talked to two male participants, but they downplayed their gender status during the interviews. Consistent with the overall trends of the platform, most of my participants were from English-speaking countries such as the United States, Canada, Australia, and Ireland. Three-fourths spoke another language in addition to English at home, and they mentioned that a secondary purpose of using Wattpad was to practice their English. At least half mentioned that writing fanfiction was not something they would discuss with their local family, peers, or teachers. Although *Directioners* often spoke of being embarrassed by their affection for the band in local contexts, their activities on Wattpad provided pathways to anonymously geek out over the band, meet like-minded fans, and connect this passion to literary and academic pursuits.

At the time of the study (2012–2013), One Direction fanfiction was the topic with the highest readership and sharing rates on Wattpad. Participants did not always know that they would become writers when they discovered the site. In fact, some of my interviewees described getting into reading and writing band fanfiction—stories about specific band members—from combing the internet for information about the band. Most of the prolific boyband authors I interviewed were girls, and within that group, most identified as "fangirls." Writing and reading boyband fanfiction was one of the ways they participated in the larger fandom, which was described interchangeably as a "family" and the "fiercest fandom" on the internet. Shared practices of commenting, advertising, helping each other, and often defending their fandom from outsiders helped foster a friendly and productive environment. Statements such as "We are a family" provide a window into the common language, identity, and purpose shared by 1D fanfiction participants on Wattpad. With these commonalities, *Directioners* on Wattpad provided feedback to each other in service of a better final product. Many participants viewed this space as communal, and they would walk the line between friendliness and criticality in their comments in order to preserve the friendship-driven spirit in the comments section.

Using the Wattpad platform and embedded tools, 1D fanfiction writers compose, share, market, and provide feedback on self-published stories. To pique the interest of their readers, authors will often release their work chapter by chapter. Freshly published chapters are peppered by comments encouraging the author to release the new chapter, and instantaneous feedback is given once the chapter arrives, varying from the positive ("wow!") to the negative ("spellcheck much?"). The site provides greater connectivity between writers, audiences, sources of information, and sites of affiliation. United by shared purposes of producing and consuming stories about the band, *Directioners* use the platform to access new content, connect to new people, gather feedback, hone their craft, and share their writing.

In addition to using the social tools on the site, *Directioners* themselves often spearhead efforts to make the platform more social. Besides using features and processes afforded by site design, they have created on-site fan clubs, provided links to fan content and external social networks (e.g., their Tumblr, Facebook, and Kik pages), and created new user accounts giving access to multiple people in order to collaborate on a specific project or series. Although the site itself posts new stories on the "New" tab and automatically emails followers, this is often not enough for budding fanfic writers in search of new audiences, greater readership, and, sometimes, votes. In addition to using the features in place, users will change their profile pictures to include memos such as "New! Hot off the presses!" and send out mass messages to let everyone know a new chapter is up. As testament to the networked writing ecology of today, *Directioners* leverage their fan networks through sites such as Tumblr and YouTube by distributing posters and movie trailers to publicize their story project. These kinds of sociability and affiliation-building aspects of Wattpad have solidified its hold as an openly networked writing platform. Authors now use mobile phones and tablets to access "their Wattpad" more often than computers: 80 percent of users report using mobile technology to access the platform (Ganglani 2014), which makes it easier for users to know when a new story is up and to respond instantly on their phones.

Although *Directioners* specialize in 1D fanfiction, their stories often incorporate features from other genres (e.g., sci-fi), characters from other content worlds (e.g., *Twilight*), and aspects of writers' personal histories. Young authors often remix genres, fandoms, and life events in the crafting of their story projects in open-ended ways. For example, you could see an e-book chapter about a blossoming romance between *Twilight*-based Bella and a 1D boyband member, but the setting of the story might be at *Harry Potter*–based Hogwarts School of Witchcraft and Wizardry. The character development of this "Bella" might come from a fellow forum visitor who had asked the author to write Bella to have a personality more like that of the fan's in real life.

Avid readers of 1D fanfiction stories would explain that to be counted as "hot," a story would need more than "quality writing," which was defined in this space as clean spelling, clever metaphors, and well-placed cliffhangers. In addition to quality writing, reach and reputation (measured by readership statistics and comment counts) became key indicators of community standing. In addition, to be held in high esteem by the fan community, the story would require correct use of slang and themes based on new developments in boyband members' lives or something from the social network of fans' lives. For instance, after a much-publicized breakup between a 1D member and another celebrity, a slew of stories explaining the breakup and what would come next followed.

One could figure out if the story were held in high esteem by looking at the number of "reads," which correlated to the possibility of appearing on the "Hot List" and the potential to win one of the sitewide Watty Awards that are given out once a year. Often, *Directioners* would refer to the authors of "hot" stories as "Wattpad celebrities," pointing to their high status among Wattpad users. The importance of the status economy (see chapter 3) came up in forum discussions and my interviews as fans tried to figure out how to gain readership or complained of vote trading that made certain users seem "better" or "hotter" than they actually were. Interviewees complained that *Directioners* often would simply trade "likes" for "likes" to increase their readership count and the chance to be featured in the contest. Instead, many argued, "likes" should signify truly liking someone's story, whether it was due to an apt knowledge of the band's history or a personal connection to the characters. To this end, *Directioners* began putting together an alternative recognition mechanism for the best story of the year. Interviewees explained that the user-organized system relied on criteria important to fans as opposed to counts of "reads" and "likes."

Because of its ability to weave different existing social networks and fan groups together, the Wattpad platform provides a way for *Directioners* to discover, develop, and capitalize on their interests. Young people active in this space are able to connect their interests grounded in pop culture to practices they see as more serious or consequential to academics and careers, such as writing, editing, and media production. New tools such as this help make the process of writing more "networked," with greater access to different sites, sources of information, and potential readers and reviewers. Internet technologies also add new avenues for inspiration, affiliation, audience management, publishing, and distribution for budding authors. Within this space, *Directioners* have come to rely on affordances of internet-mediated writing, such as consistent communication, prompt feedback, and integration of existing social networks.

Learner Story

Interests in popular culture, when aided by strong social supports, may become gateways for young people to engage in meaningful literacy practices. Abigail, a white 13-year-old author from Canada, got involved in Wattpad when she and her siblings received a mobile phone to share on her 12th birthday. Right away, she was drawn into the fanfiction section of Wattpad because her favorite band (1D) and her favorite movie series (*Harry Potter*) were the most popular topics. In addition to housing stories on her favorite topics, she liked that this genre used collaborative accounts that provided a way to start writing and publishing without tying the final products to her user name. She thought that this was a less stressful way to experiment with writing. She had not dabbled in creative writing before this, and she was experiencing performance anxiety: "I was nervous. I was afraid people would judge me and post hate comments and I would have to defend my own work. It was the exact opposite! People loved my work and they were supportive." Through participating in these "collab" accounts, Abigail was able to rehearse and polish her writing skills. By collaborating with seasoned writers, she was able to learn the ins and outs of fanfiction writing as a genre.

Abigail explains that the support of her teachers and family was essential to perseverance as a young self-publishing author. She said that "[her] English teacher and drama teacher both know and are very supportive" of her work on Wattpad, which she shares with them. In fact, both her mom and her English teacher provide encouragement for her writing. In this way, Abigail's out-of-school literacy practices are supported by her family, a representative of the school, and fellow members of the community. Through mechanisms of support, Wattpad fan communities, just like specific family members of participants, broker the ways in which participants see their involvement on the fan site as consequential to other contexts, such as school, clubs, and even possible career pathways.

As Abigail gained followers and standing within the fanfiction community, she also gained a sense of experience and self-efficacy with writing that informed her school life. She explains that whenever she had free-form writing time in middle school, her Wattpad experiences helped her with creativity. In addition to her writing skills' being nurtured by her writing partners on Wattpad, Abigail points out changes in disposition toward writing as a practice. She no longer has trouble with fear of critique now that she is a practiced writer. She has developed a feel for creating stories and filling in plot holes; storytelling has become second nature. As she puts it, being a seasoned author helps her both on Wattpad and in English class at school: "Experience with [fanfic] made me think of ideas and helped them flow better and write better than I could have before." Inspired and bolstered by her success on Wattpad, Abigail recently applied and got into a selective creative writing program at a magnet school. Her mother explains that this is no small feat: The magnet school is quite far from their house and is male dominated, and most of Abigail's childhood friends are going to the local public school. Abigail remains unafraid: "Wattpad [writing] encouraged me to expand on my talents. I would actually like to be a writer now! It has made me more optimistic in a way." With the help of peer support, a production-centered hobby, and help at home, Abigail was able to connect her passions for specific content worlds to concrete academic and professional opportunities.

Bollywood Dance

Sangita Shresthova

I pretty much went on YouTube and started watching other
dancers and videos of dance performances, dance teams,
dance crews so on and so forth.[1] I watched all that stuff. . . .
I started dancing in an empty motel room somewhere [in a
motel my parents owned]. I had these old Dell speakers that
I plugged in and just jammed out. . . . I did that for a while.
That's pretty much how I grew into dancing.

In his interview, Rohit, age 22 and living in North Carolina,[2] shared his
early dance memories. Inspired by Indian dance shows such as *Dance
India Dance* on Zee TV and Hindi (Bollywood) films he watched with
his parents as a child in the United States, he started his dance education
in the privacy of unoccupied rooms of the motel his parents operated.
His first performance took place at his cousin's wedding and was a huge
success. As Rohit's interest in dance grew, his friends and relatives sent
dance videos his way until he eventually learned about the fast-growing
competitive Bollywood dance teams on college campuses all over the
United States (including universities such as Northwestern University
in Chicago; see figure C.2.2). He joined the team on his campus his freshman year and went on to compete in, and even judge, many competitions
and performances. He has now become a prominent, connected, and visible member of the competitive Bollywood dance community, which is
part of a participatory Bollywood dance culture that grew out of global
circulation of Hindi films over the past two decades.

About Bollywood Dance and Competitions

Bollywood dance typically refers to dances set to Hindi film songs. These
dances may appear in the films themselves, and they may also be live

Figure C.2.2. Anubhav, Northwestern University's Bollywood dance team, performs in 2014. Image courtesy of Carlo Cruz/MSTRCRZ Photography.

performances inspired by these films. While dances in Hindi films have existed for almost a century, it was the 1990s that witnessed the rise of Bollywood dance as a distinct global style. As digital media enabled a more prolific peer-to-peer circulation of Hindi films, Bollywood dance became an even more common occurrence at South Asian get-togethers and parties among Indian diasporic communities. Dance schools that teach the hippest Bollywood dances soon opened in many cities. Today, Bollywood dance still thrives as a popular and largely participatory dance, which invites fans to perform their love for Bollywood films as they also change and augment choreography to make it their own.

Dancers I met during my earlier research in the United States (Shresthova 2011) often described their initial Bollywood dance experience as akin to "taking lessons in Indianness." To them Bollywood dance became a practice that allowed them to keep up with narratives in Hindi films. Learning to execute the dance movements they contained also helped them connect with their ethnic and cultural backgrounds as second-generation Indian Americans. At the same time, these dancers were often quick to distinguish between the more formally constrained and culturally conservative lessons offered through the study of India's classical dance forms (such as Bharatanatyam and Kathak) and the more flexible and permissive approach to choreography and movement creation they found through Bollywood dance. Like the dances in Hindi films, which from their inception drew on a range of Indian and non-Indian dance traditions (see Rao 1995), live Bollywood dance is best described as an inherently hybrid dance form that draws on an ever-changing repertoire of dance styles to create and express meaningful emotions and narratives. Live Bollywood dancers actively tap this hybridity to shape their own dance experiences.

Bollywood competition dancers claim full ownership over Bollywood's rootedness in Indian culture. They also tap its hybrid nature as they create choreography that draws on their Indian heritage while simultaneously drawing on themes that grow out of their experience as second-generation Indian Americans. The dancers I spoke with recognized this dual role for Bollywood dance in their community. One female dancer thought that Bollywood dance was "a way to connect with [Indian] culture so to learn more about what was going on in the Bollywood scene and things like that, but also connecting with different people"—most of the people on the team are Indian. To her, being part of a team allowed her to "reconnect with that whole area" of her life. Other dancers similarly saw exposure to Bollywood films and choreography as a way to gain more exposure to their Indian heritage.

Other dancers identified the cultural porousness within Bollywood as crucial to their involvement with the scene. Pointing to diversity within the film industry, Rajesh, a dancer based on the East Coast, observed that dancers involved in dance competitions are probably most drawn to the "creative side of Bollywood itself," which makes it "easy to relate to for everyone as opposed to any traditional [dance] style." With an increasingly tight-knit connection between live and filmed Bollywood dances, we can speak about what I have previously called a "symbiotic relationship" between dances in Hindi films and live Bollywood dance choreography, in which Hindi film choreographers simultaneously follow and influence live Bollywood dance trends (Shresthova 2011:151–53).

The affordances of new media further reinforce this symbiotic relationship and support the communities of practice that have emerged around it. As Hindi films and videos of live Bollywood dance performances circulate online in an openly networked environment, both become more accessible to a wider range of fans and choreographers. These affinities between filmed and live Bollywood dance are crucial to the meanings these dances create. For one, local choreographers do not always simply "copy" movements. Many of them take great pride in appropriating, adjusting, and at times completely changing existing Bollywood choreography to reflect local aesthetics and contexts. New dances, performances, and classes spread through social media. Bollywood dance online access has also been significant for choreographers in the industry, who come into more direct contact with live fan-driven interpretations of their choreography. New media have clearly supported the growth of Bollywood dance as a participatory performative site of cultural appropriation that bridges local and online spaces.

The Bollywood dance competition scene on U.S. college and university campuses is an outgrowth of Bollywood dance as a popular participatory dance style, with the addition of competition as a motivating factor and shared purpose. While Bollywood dance competitions owe much to Bollywood's popularity, they also build on a longer tradition of other Indian dance–style competitions, such as Bhangra and Raas, which focus on folk dances associated with particular regions in India. Although no "official" registry of Bollywood (also referred to as Hindi Film Dance or HFD) competitions and teams exists, it is a space that is still clearly experiencing significant growth. As Rohit observed, "Every year as the competition increased the [choreographic] cleanliness of the teams increased, the energy of the teams increased." Bollywood dance teams now exist on many (if not most) large and medium-sized college campuses. Once a team is established, its team members set out to "get it on the map" by submitting applications to existing competitions. Organized by recent alumni from competitive teams, the competitions vary in focus: Some stress choreography; others look at the whole performance and recognize that props and costumes are a key element of performance. Competitions also vary from regional to national. As a rule of thumb, the broader the geographical range, the more prestigious a competition becomes. New and less-known teams often celebrate placing in a competition as a significant accomplishment.

In 2010, *Bollywood America* was established by recent Bollywood competition alumni to become the first national championship for college

Bollywood dance teams. While it is difficult to estimate the scale of the Bollywood dance competitive scene, it is safe to say that it involves thousands of young people across college campuses in the United States who keep in touch with each other through networks that rely heavily on new and social media. Competition organizers circulate application packets through Facebook groups. Peer reviews of competition performances and choreography are (often vehemently) debated on desidanceteams.com, a website hub where much publicly accessible information about the scene resides. For example, the question of what constitutes "authentic" and "original" choreography for Bollywood dance emerges as a recurring topic, and it is often tied to debates around what, if any, formal connection the Bollywood dance scene has to the Hindi film industry. It also touches on how this emergent Indian American dance scene can continue to break away from being "derivative" of dances contained in Hindi films to assume a life of its own. As these discussions evolve, the teams move toward a fuller expression of the hyphenated experiences of being American *and* Indian (or, more broadly, South Asian).

Bollywood Dance Teams as Learning Communities

The broader context of the intercollegiate competition network frames how local teams operate and organize. Given the competitive nature of the scene, team members audition to join teams. More experienced and senior dancers generally rise through the ranks to assume leadership (captain and lead dancer) roles, which gives them more decision-making powers when it comes to deciding on competition applications, rehearsal schedules, and choreographic priorities. That said, the dancers I interviewed overwhelmingly stressed peer-to-peer learning and participation as key for the teams' operations, which include fundraising, rehearsals, creating videos, mixing sound, costume making, prop development, and people management.

Dance teams adopt a range of approaches toward providing help and feedback that is timely, constructive, and driven by the specific demands of their group's practice. Neesha, based in California, explained that she taught herself how to use GarageBand because her team needed a sound mix. Initially, she reached out to other team members for help, but eventually she got so good at it that others now approach her for advice.

This demand-driven approach to learning within teams also encourages innovative approaches to problem solving. Jaya, from Illinois, recalled how she decided to use video as an integral part of the rehearsal process for her team: "I quickly realized that if I told someone, 'Your hand isn't straight, it's at a diagonal,' they felt as though it was straight. But as soon as I would record them, they would see it with their own eyes. . . . So I think recording it was a very good tool because people could actually see what was needed to be improved."

Jaya began a practice of recording documentary video and posting on the team's private Facebook group so team members could watch and comment, enabling a peer-to-peer feedback mechanism that was both effective and participatory.

All the dance teams I encountered had a private Facebook group (or other similar social media mechanism). They used this forum to surface ideas related to performance choreography and theme, and they often circulated existing Bollywood and other dance videos for inspiration. The team members would then collectively comment on what they noticed, liked, and thought might be changed. Many teams also used privately circulated videos as a tool for creating, rehearsing, and document-ing choreography. Like Jaya, they used video to provide feedback on rehearsals. The dancers thought digital and social media were just as im-portant as the in-person rehearsal and meeting sessions for their teams.

In addition to dance and choreography skills, dancers also picked up other skills as part of their participation in their shared practices. Nee-sha recalled the moment when she realized that running a Bollywood dance team is "basically running a business," in which 17- to 22-year-olds need to figure out how to "delegate things" and take on "certain respon-sibilities." Other dancers thought they had acquired important skills in areas such as fundraising (to cover the cost of costumes and travel to competitions), teamwork (setting up goals, getting things done), pro-duction (prop making, video editing), marketing (getting word out about performances), and online research (finding videos, learning about Bollywood dance). Those who had graduated from college often drew on their experience with Bollywood dance during interviews. Anil, who is an engineering major and grew up in Chicago, explains: "That's my main thing that I really try to talk about because that's who I am. It shaped so much who I am. It may seem hard to compare engineering and dancing: how do you compare the two? But . . . being in a world space you have to be able to apply the kind of things that I learnt from the dancing as well."

Learner Story

Before he started university in Northern California (where he grew up), Akash did not think about dance as a serious pastime. Now that he is a senior majoring in biomedical engineering, Akash sees his dancing, specifically dancing with Prakasha, the competitive Bollywood dance team on his university campus, as an extremely important interest-driven activity. He thinks being part of the team helped him build unexpected skills while also providing him with many friendships, which form a community of support that has helped him become more consciously aware of his identity as a second-generation American of Indian origin.

Established in 2011, Prakasha is a competitive dance team focused on competing in the emergent Bollywood or HFD competition circuit. Both the team and the scene have continued to grow steadily during the past decade. Enabled overwhelmingly through the digital circulation of both dances contained in Hindi films and the Bollywood dances they inspire, the HFD competitions build on a globally thriving Bollywood dance culture.

Akash remembers that he was not very athletic when he was a child and that his parents were eager to find something that would move his body. This was how he ended up taking dance classes, mostly because his sister was already enrolled in them. He dropped out after a few years and did not think about dance much until his freshman year in college. Encouraged by a friend, he decided to audition for Prakasha, but he admits he probably got in because "it's not very difficult" for male dancers, as the Bollywood dance teams are always "looking for guys to join."

Akash first focused on mastering dance moves and memorizing choreography. Through peer-run rehearsals several times a week that often ran late into the night, he soon ramped up his movement abilities. Within a year, he branched out into creating choreography for the team. Akash draws his inspiration from YouTube hip-hop dance videos that he and his teammates share with each other through closed-group discussions on social media (predominantly Facebook) more than from

Bollywood films and the dances contained in them. In fact, exchanging videos, along with commentary on dance movements and choreography, is a key activity for team members. Akash describes how "most of our [team] communication happens online through texting apps or through Facebook." These YouTube videos, online team exchanges, and in-person rehearsals are where he has learned what he knows about dance composition and choreography, an area in which he never had any formal studio-based dance training.

Dance creation and rehearsals account for only part of what young people commit to when they join Prakasha. Team members are also responsible for identifying, organizing, and completing all the tasks needed for a successful collegiate Bollywood dance season. This includes fundraising, costume making, sound mixing, and creating videos documenting rehearsals. For Akash, building props and creating short films that introduce the team's performances (a requirement for most competitions) emerged as areas of interest and continued skill development. Given his mechanical engineering focus, Akash sees being in charge of prop building for Prakasha as an extension of his professional training, and as something that allows him to build connections between his dancing and his engineering major. He recalls that he constructed a tank during his first year on the team, which became a prop that put his newly established team on the Bollywood competition map: "We actually get judged for what props we bring out and how we use them. So my first year, I designed a tank. We had a military theme to our dance and so I designed this huge tank. We had five people sitting inside of it and it would roll out on the stage that had wheels and the top thing would rotate with the cannon and then five people would jump out from inside out of it. I designed and built the whole thing myself."

Digging deeper into the specifics, Akash notes that building props for the team forces him to apply his engineering skills to meet functional demands. For example, when he built a large frame for another performance, he faced a "pretty big challenge" in finding a way to make the frame "light enough to drag out on the stage and then immediately drag back off stage and still support all the choreo that they're doing inside."

In addition to building props, Akash has also become the designated filmmaker for Prakasha. He is in charge of all the videos the team creates, particularly the short introductory videos that come before competitive appearances, introduce the team, and set up the performance thematically. Akash, who has never taken a film class, looks to existing films and media he finds online for inspiration. He explains: "Sometimes I'll just see something and be like there is no better way they could have filmed that. . . . Other times I'll be watching, I don't know like a TV show, like Arrow or something and I'll say they could have done that from a different angle . . . and they would have gotten the same message across." Akash also looks to other filmmakers in the Bollywood competition network. He keeps up with what they create and exchanges ideas with them regularly.

Such exchanges are part of the peer support and friendship that Akash found through Prakasha, which to him is first and foremost "a group of people that I can go out with, have fun with, I can connect to." Overwhelmingly, the community draws on many members' shared experiences as second-generation Indian Americans, whom many (including Akash) jokingly refer to as ABCDs, or "American Born Confused Desis." "Desis" is a colloquial term used to describe people from the Indian subcontinent. While Akash does not see his involvement with Prakasha as explicitly political, he does assign significance to the sense of shared collective identity that gets supported through the Bollywood dance scene. He explains that the dances inspired by Bollywood films become the foundation for exploration of cultural and civic issues, which most recently included surfacing intergenerational conflicts around LGBTQ issues within Indian American communities.

Moving forward, Akash has been selected to be one of Prakasha's captains and will assume even more responsibilities on the team. At the time of the interview, Akash was busy preparing for the upcoming year, filling out forms to reserve rooms. He was also in the midst of collaborating with his co-captains to create choreography and plan auditions that would bring new members into the team as soon as classes resumed. Though he does not see himself pursuing a dance-related career, he, like the other dancers I interviewed, thought that the skills he had picked up through Bollywood dance would serve him well in years to come.

3

Status

Developing Social and Cultural Capital

Lead Author: Matthew H. Rafalow

Introduction

Lauren Chicoine[1] discovered her love for anime in college, but only upon entering an online anime music video (AMV) community did she find a passion for creating her own digital movies (see the case study at the end of this chapter for more on AMV creation). "I had once seen an awesome *Final Fantasy 8* AMV and was fascinated by it," she explained. She "became obsessed" when she stumbled on the online community. "I was just like . . . oh my God! I, too, can realize my creative vision!" For Lauren, her excitement was intimately connected to social aspects of making. She wanted "to tell a story, to share something that's in my head with other people." Lauren had to learn how to use Adobe Premier and After Effects as part of the AMV creation process, a challenging learning experience that, in her words, "kicked me in the butt." Lauren decided to give back to the community by sharing some of the skills she had learned as a graphic designer. She created tutorials for various techniques and tools in Photoshop, in areas that she saw other AMV editors struggling with. Over time, Lauren became recognized in the community for her sophisticated use of design elements and techniques in her videos, as well as her helpful tutorials. Other editors would contact her personally for advice and feedback, and she was even featured in an interview series published on the AMV site because of some of these unique techniques she employed.

Lauren's process of "leveling up" in the AMV online community illustrates how learning and achievement are tied to relationships and status cultivated in an online affinity network. In the previous chapter we described the glue—shared interests, affinities, purposes, and practices—that holds online affinity groups together. This chapter focuses on the chisel—how networks delineate membership, status, and achievement, and how young people navigate these social and cultural distinctions. While all the online affinity networks we studied are openly networked and have low barriers to entry, they also have ways of marking boundaries, status, and hierarchy. In order to be both open and maintain high standards, they must enforce community norms, reward individual contributions, and mark quality work. As youth become more embedded in the online affinity networks we studied, they gain skill and cultural know-how, and they build new relationships centered on learning and co-mentorship in their area of interest. Unlike social networks that young people navigate in their schools, families, and local peer groups, the relationships formed in online affinity networks are more tuned to a particular identity, interest, or purpose. When focused on expertise and cultural production, these specialized networks and relationships fuel learning by providing knowledge, support, and feedback. The relationships and learning in online affinity networks are powerful but also compartmentalized in ways that are both liberating and limiting because of disconnection from relationships and organizations in young people's local communities. After first framing how we conceptualize the unique forms of cultural capital that young people gain through online affinity networks, we delve into the details of how community norms, reputation, and status are negotiated and the implications for learning.

Subcultural Capital and Learning in Online Affinity Networks

Online affinity networks confer unique benefits—membership and status within a specialized network as well as access to learning-relevant assets such as coveted information, helpful feedback, and visibility. We draw on long-standing educational research that has investigated how cultural and social capital—understood as valuable cultural status and social connections—relates to learning and opportunity (Bourdieu 1986; J. Coleman 1988; Horvat, Weininger, and Lareau 2003). Unlike most strands of work in this area, however, our focus is not on the cultural and social capital that accrues in dominant organizations such as schools, civic institutions, and workplaces. Instead, our focus is more aligned with what Sarah Thornton (1996) has described as "subcultural capital" within the underground music scene.

Research on youth subcultures argues that they emerge, in part, through an act of resistance to mainstream society (Brake 2003; Hebdige 1979; Wilkins 2008). Further, youth subcultures are not monolithic; they shape, and are shaped by, the contexts in which youth interact with others (McRobbie 1994). The networks we studied share many of these characteristics, but they lack the active opposition to mainstream or middle-class culture of the prototypical subcultural frame. Instead, they are more akin to what Stephen Duncombe (2008) described in his study of DIY zine publishers, a nerdy "alternative culture" that is more "subterranean" or "underground" than oppositional. In describing otaku culture in the United States, Lawrence Eng suggests that "their resistance is oblique, based on appropriation rather than rejection of media and other technology that they fundamentally enjoy" (Eng 2012:100). While many online affinity networks do have more oppositional qualities, our cases also tended toward these more nerdy and less oppositional cultural valences. Fandoms and online affinity networks point to the unbundling of some of the associations ascribed to subcultures; we use the term "subcultural capital" with the caveat that our groups do not conform to the classic oppositional frame associated with the term.

Where our cases found common cause with the longer history of youth subculture studies is in their distinctive forms of insider knowledge and status markers that distinguish them from mainstream culture and dominant social networks. Participants typically reflect that they do not have local networks through which to pursue the interests that are celebrated in these online affinity networks. We also found that the online affinity networks we examined require that new members acquire subcultural capital to fully participate. As youth discover and join online affinity networks to pursue their interests in video games, boybands, wrestling, or knitting, they interface with etiquette, social norms, and rituals that are initially quite foreign to them. Learning-centered online affinity networks have processes for welcoming newcomers and educating them in community-specific know-how, ways for people to seek and give feedback, and status systems that reward experienced members for their demonstrations of skill.

Examining the relationship between subcultural capital and connected learning calls attention to how learning and achievement are supported by specific forms of cultural identity, relationships, and social networks. By using the language of cultural and social capital, we do not imply that value accrues in a universal and linear way as young people build their social networks and cultural competence. Instead, we see what counts as culturally and socially valuable as under constant negotiation and contention, and it can be challenging to convert value between different subcultures or in ways recognized by mainstream institutions. High status in a science-fiction fandom does not necessarily translate to status among athletes or school-based achievement. Young people are being socialized into new systems of social and cultural value as they enter new online affinity networks, and they can struggle to make these values and relationships intelligible to parents, teachers, and peers in their local communities. Our earlier Digital Youth Project research reported on how young people "segmented" their identities, creating separate online identities for nerdy affinity networks that were firewalled from their school-based identities displayed on Facebook or MySpace accounts (Ito et al. 2010). As more young people report making new friendships online (Lenhart et al. 2015), we expect that these experiences of navigating varied regimes of social, cultural, and subcultural capital will become increasingly commonplace.

The subcultural capital cultivated by online affinity networks has qualities associated with "bonding social capital"—relationships that develop among groups of people who share similar interests or circumstances—which is associated with high levels of social cohesion, shared norms, trust, information sharing, help, and support (Portes and Landolt 1996; Woolcock 1998). A classic example of bonding capital appears in Putnam's (2001) discussion of American bowling leagues, where he finds that participation is associated with greater group solidarity, support, and even safe spaces for participants to reflect on society and civic affairs. While scant work examines the relationship between bonding social capital and young people's education, some learning scientists suggest that bonded relationships among members of a learning community may lead to greater information sharing, trust, and support among students (Daniel, Schwier, and McCalla 2003). We find, too, that bonded relationships are critical to youth participants in online affinity networks for leveling up as learners.

In an extension of the concept of bonding social capital, Mario Small (2009) examined the development of bonding social capital as well as its benefits in a study of day-care centers in New York City. Unlike the layered and multifaceted relationships that Putnam identified in bowling clubs or church groups, the relationships fostered in day-care centers that Small describes are bonded and supportive relationships largely contained within the specific sphere of child rearing. He refers to these organization-driven types of connections as "compartmental intimates." For example, Small shows how parents help one another, for example, by babysitting each other's children, gifting baby clothes, or sharing tips about treating childhood illnesses. These relationships did not exist separately from the parents' overlapping participation at the child-care center, and thus they provided a compartmentalized yet quite intimate type of relationship with key benefits. We find that the social capital that youth develop in online affinity networks is similarly specialized and compartmentalized. Although different from the parents in Small's study who come together for the mutual need for child care, the social networks in youth online affinity networks share this close but compartmentalized quality.

The everyday activities of online affinity networks, including forum discussions, contests, and member-organized classes, provide a setting where youth can develop strong bonds with peers who help them and cheer them on as they level up. They contrast with the status systems of freaks, geeks, and cool kids, jocks, and burnouts, situated in schools where youth are not likely to be voluntary participants (Eckert 1989; Milner 2013). As we saw in the previous chapter, youth find and participate in online affinity networks voluntarily because they are seeking a network of peers with shared interests and affinities. Many of our respondents explain that they enjoy participating in their online affinity network because they are recognized for work activities related to their interests that are not seen as valuable at school. This does not mean, however, that online affinity networks are devoid of hierarchy and exclusions. Ito (2012a) finds that AMV or video remix fans develop their own norms, status hierarchies, and boundary-making processes around a noncommercial, amateur ethos aimed at inclusivity while also cultivating an insider subcultural identity. Similarly, Schor et al. (2015) find that seemingly open-access peer-to-peer sharing communities can require rarified forms of cultural capital for full participation. Somewhat ironically, these informal social and cultural ways of marking status take on more salience in openly networked systems that lack formal organizational roles and hierarchies.

These themes are similar to norm formation in other online settings, such as usenet forums or chats, for which researchers have described barriers to entry for newcomers (Burnett and Bonnici 2003; Cherny 1999). We have sought out networks that do not have overtly exclusionary values. For example, while still male dominated, the gaming networks we studied show little evidence of the overt sexism that characterizes #gamergate. Still, the insider knowledge, cultural referents, and technical knowledge of these groups make them less welcoming to those not immersed in male-dominated gaming culture. The specialization and bonding of online affinity networks necessarily creates distinctions between insiders and outsiders.

The remainder of this chapter describes the dynamics of how the online affinity networks we studied enforce norms, encourage mentorship, and mark status, and then it explores implications for learning. In line with the overall aim of our book to surface the potential for online affinity networks to support connected learning, we focus on how groups maintain standards, and how active participants work to meet them. How do new members develop the subcultural capital needed to navigate these systems of achievement? How do participants learn community norms for talk and interactions with others, and what is considered transgressive and counterproductive to the social order? And if participants learn from others, how do they find those mentors—and where do those teachers come from? After first describing the ways in which the online affinity networks we studied enforce and support community norms and standards, the chapter describes the learning-relevant benefits of participation—mentorship, feedback, and specialized knowledge.

Status Systems

In all of our case studies, various forms of status systems operate within their respective learning environments. Much like prior work on youth subcultures, we find that each community arranges membership across key status classifications (Ito 2012a; Thornton 1996). In what follows, we discuss these systems in three parts: status recognition processes tied to affinity network participation, elites as status exemplars, and the roles of mentors and peers in teaching and conferring subcultural capital.

Learning and Earning Subcultural Capital

In this section we highlight the entry points for new participants to show how each community maintains its own distinct set of rules, expectations, and protocols. These norms and understandings of participation are invisible and unknown to those who are new to the online affinity network. New participants must be socialized into the workings of the affinity network's subcultural capital and the knowledge and dispositions needed to successfully navigate the affinity network.

At *Hogwarts at Ravelry*, participants create a learning environment in the image of Hogwarts, the magical school of the *Harry Potter* series (see figure 3.1; the case study appears at the end of chapter 4). Community members organize creative production around elaborate houses with their own rules, hierarchies, and traditions. New members are sorted into four distinct houses—Gryffindor, Ravenclaw, Hufflepuff, and Slytherin—each with its own "common room" thread in the forums. Although people can join the Hogwarts community at any time, they are sorted into houses only during "sort" weeks, or weeks between class rotations. Roughly every six weeks there is a one-week sort period. To fully participate, members must become familiar with *Harry Potter* lore and language, sometimes even role-playing in ways that demonstrate familiarity with the series. For example, Jen2291,[2] a 49-year-old white woman from Arizona, participated in an Order of the Phoenix game within *Hogwarts at Ravelry* that organized challenges centered on creative writing. In one of her submissions, she wrote about her family background as a descendant of "Antioch Peverell" and a family who was fascinated with "muggles." Her career aspirations, she notes, include becoming an "auror" as a result of her disgust for evil "Death Eaters." She concludes by discussing her special talents for "transfiguration" and her experiences fighting "Dementors." Understanding and engaging with Jen2291's shared writing, as well as other activities, such as role-playing and lessons, requires extensive knowledge of the fandom.

Established rules and etiquette for classes offered through *Hogwarts at Ravelry* must be mastered for participants to forge ahead. New

Figure 3.1. Screen shot of *Hogwarts at Ravelry*'s main page.
Image from Ravelry.com.

members often feel intimidated when they first join the community because of the large number of activities and the school-oriented metaphor
for participation. New participants must join classes and earn points by
submitting their own crafted items and patterns, thus filtering out people who are not serious about joining. Teachers also award bonus points
to students who design their own patterns and build their own shapes
from scratch. In addition to these established structures for activity and
lessons, fandom-centered lore, and formulae for earning points, there
are restrictions on the form and content of communications on the forums that include keeping discussion "G"-rated and not being overly
critical of others' projects. Although *Hogwarts at Ravelry* and the other
affinity networks we studied provide various mechanisms to guide new
members through their systems for participation, this example shows
the many different rules, procedures, linguistic and fandom-related
knowledge, and expectations for appropriate communications that are
typically unknown to those outside of the subculture.

The *StarCraft II* community also requires considerable gameplay
and technical know-how to be able to fully participate (the case study

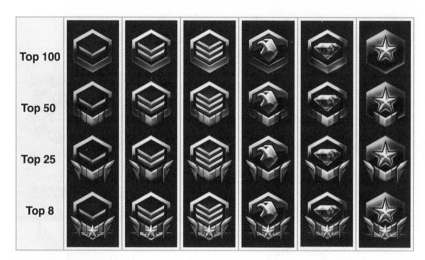

Figure 3.2. *StarCraft II* players compete and climb rankings.
Image from Liquipedia.

appears at the end of chapter 1). As in other complex, competitive games, the learning curve to competency is steep, both cognitively and physically, and elite gamer culture is famously exclusionary. Proficiency in the game requires advanced cognitive capacities for multitasking and problem solving (Glass, Maddox, and Love 2013), as well as lightning-fast physical reflexes, which gamers measure as an "actions per minute" (APM) score (see figure 3.2 for an example of *StarCraft II* rankings). In addition to performance in the game, players must become fluent and comfortable in the arcane lingua franca and norms of gamer culture as they navigate forums and in-game chat and converse on shared audio channels. Game strategy, terms, and the latest news on various tournaments and players are chronicled through thousands of forums, wikis, and videos. Even to be a competent spectator of an esport such as *StarCraft II* requires considerable knowledge that is outside the scope of nongamers. Even with a competent screencaster offering commentary, outsiders will find it challenging to understand even the basics of how the match is progressing.

Sackboy Planet, like many online environments, is an attention-scarce marketplace for social exchange (see the case study at the end of this chapter). Because of the incredibly high volume of content and means through which to interact with other *LBP2* players, participants expect that any communications meet certain standards before getting either supportive feedback or any responses at all. These expectations are also not clear to outsiders and must be learned through time. For example, one player reflected that people who are often ignored are those who write only in capital or lowercase letters: "If they're like 'ZOMGZ PLAY MY LEVELZ PLZ! YOU WILL LOVE IT! OMG!' All lower case, run on sentences." People who communicate in ways that do not use proper forms of English grammar, or who are overly demanding and repeatedly comment or spam the forums, are often characterized by experienced members as "immature children." As a consequence, those who communicate in these ways often get skipped over or ignored and are effectively squelched from participation. These dialogic expectations are closely tied to success in the formal metrics that operate in the game and in *Sackboy Planet*. For budding designers to get others to play and review their levels, and to have a shot at earning "likes" or "hearts," which are among the highest markers of success, community members must be willing to take requests for feedback seriously. If they overtly ask for likes or hearts, or if they demand that people look at their creations without introducing themselves and making an effort to get to know people first, they are stifled from meaningful participation on the road to improving their craft and leveling up.

Directioners on the Wattpad online publishing platform must also learn the appropriate etiquette for sharing feedback on others' writing if they wish to fully participate (see the end of chapter 2 for the 1D on Wattpad case study). One example of this etiquette is to provide only constructive suggestions; to do otherwise would be a violation of "friend behavior" mandated by the community. For example, Madeleine, a 15-year-old white teen from Canada, explained that "if you aren't nice to people, no one will stick up for you if you are insulted." She reflects that when evaluating others' work, she makes sure she offers supportive comments first: "I would say, 'Great job, I'm really looking forward to the next Chapter! You're a great writer! Just be sure to fix the . . . But other than that it's perfect!'" This etiquette is embedded in the subculture among *Directioners* on Wattpad and must be learned upon entry.

Similarly, professional wrestling community members (see the *Wrestling Boards* case study at the end of chapter 1) must learn a number of different rules to participate, and as in *Hogwarts at Ravelry* they must demonstrate their knowledge of the fandom, including the history of wrestling, key contenders, and various terms and nuanced protocols for wrestling matches. Successful participation in the forums also requires following standards for rating and evaluating others' work, which shapes whether participants' own work is evaluated and sped along as they learn their craft and level up in the community. For example, participants are expected to rate and evaluate a certain number of shows each week. If their written feedback is too minimal, or is written in a tone considered unacceptable, then they and their work fall in social standing and they have fewer opportunities to participate in matches. Farooq, an 18-year-old African American male from San Diego and a respected member of the community, explains: "This forum isn't sugar coated, people will say what they like, or dislike. And you can tell when someone posts. This is an example of a post by a respected member: 'I agree that CM Punk is good at the mic, but he is overrated in the ring.' This is an example of a post by a non-respected member: 'Fuck CM Punk, he's good at the mic because he is a whining bitch, and he is shit in the ring.' Respected members give fair ratings to all wrestlers and hesitate from using immature insults."

Although the *Wrestling Boards* community's expectations for quality evaluations establish a safe environment for constructive feedback, its rules, understandings, and community-specific knowledge—like those in our other cases—are typically unknown to those who are outsiders to the subculture and are new to participation. Next, we describe the various reputation processes within online affinity networks that members must both reproduce and navigate to participate.

Online Reputation Systems

Many of the online affinity networks we studied include design features that denote status and reputation. We typically found that the competitive gaming communities in our study had among the most robust reputation and ranking systems because of the fact that competition and status go hand in hand. For example, members of the professional wrestling community the *Wrestling Boards* have symbols next to users' profiles that showcase whether they have "Legend" status or not.

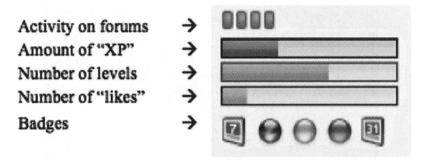

Figure 3.3. Screen shot of *Sackboy Planet* forum ratings, including badges (bottom) for participation.

According to participants, Legend status indicates to the community that these users have a long history with professional wrestling and participate frequently, and that their posts are upvoted. In the forums, people can like others' content in order to improve those users' "reps," or reputations. Reputation points are awarded by people who read a post and think it is interesting, funny, or worth attention. These different points that reflect users' reps are accumulated in a database and displayed in ways that reflect a level of status. Similarly, *Sackboy Planet* hosts a number of different metrics (refer to figure 3.3) that represent a kind of gamification of community experience intended to drive interest and persistence and to create a shared set of benchmarks. These metrics include reputation bars that reflect experience on the website, hearts for high quality levels, and likes for comments.

In the *Hogwarts at Ravelry* community, badges are awarded to participants who create official stores for their wares or to people who share exemplary work during their instructional lessons, such as completing classes and challenges (see example badge in figure 3.4). The *Hogwarts at Ravelry* community also uses a competitive point system called "house points" that parallels the *Harry Potter* series. Through this system, members are awarded points for completing lessons or doing community-valued activities such as designing their own craft patterns or giving items to charities.

In addition to explicit metrics, participants also engage in discursive strategies to improve their own status and to evaluate that of others in the community. On *Sackboy Planet*, players regularly share their

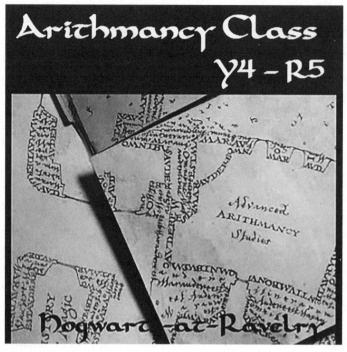

Figure 3.4. A badge for completing an arithmancy class.
Image courtesy of Myriam.

projects-in-development in a section of the forums devoted to feed-back on users' levels. The forums offer different privacy settings that allow players to bring the kind of attention they want to their products as they gain legitimacy in the community. For example, Luchadoro, a 21-year-old from the United States, was working on a level that had a lot of bugs, and he did not want to share it in a way that everyone would see just yet. But he did want feedback, and so in this early stage of develop-ment he used privacy settings on his level to allow only the people he wanted to test it. Luchadoro strategically used the privacy settings in the forums to mediate how others evaluated his work as it was improved. *LBP2* players such as Luchadoro recognize that sharing their creations affects their own standing in the community through how they navigate status systems that involve peer-to-peer evaluation of level creations.

Another example of community status processes can be found through the "booking" system among *Wrestling Boards* writers. Participants in this community must be committed to their craft through the writing and feedback systems in the forums. If writers are not active and do not write, rate, and provide extensive feedback on others' posts, their characters or writing are not "booked" for the next show. The standards for booking vary, but they center on impressing other evaluators based on shared expectations of the writing and often require good grammar and demonstrated understanding of the activity guidelines. But if participants meet these standards and their characters are cited in the grand narrative of the fight matches, it is considered a great honor. For example, one participant left feedback on another's write-up of a character: "It's AWESOME! Hopefully James Hammer will be in the next PPV!" To be selected for the upcoming match is a signal by the community that one's work is high quality.

Status systems within the online affinity networks we examined are durable and are reproduced by participants because they all share a stake in how they function. Status in the One Direction fandom on Wattpad is a complex interaction of platform-based metrics and official competitions, as well as community-driven feedback and "likes." Some participants leave comments that are defaming, such as calling others' work "fluff" publicly, and others leave benign or innocuous comments that many participants see as an attempt to game the formal status system. For One Direction fanfiction on Wattpad, the visibility and popularity of created work is increased if there are more comments. If created work reaches the highest level of popularity, those users have a shot at winning the annual Watty Awards that recognize the best work. Participants value substantive feedback and criticize as "unethical" any attempts to increase popularity through "vote trading" and false praise. However, the relationship between feedback and status can also work to support positive learning dynamics, such as through the shared expectation to give honest and constructive feedback. One writer, Ayush, a 19-year-old from India now living in Illinois, gave another writer good feedback on a story. In return, that writer gave helpful feedback on his own write-up.

So far we have described how online affinity networks contain complex subcultures with their own etiquettes and rules, as well as reputational systems that provide members the means through which to evaluate others' work and confer status. Next, we describe the key role that the highest-status participants play by creating ideals for learning and making.

Elites and Aspirational Standards

Examples of elite participants in our networks make clear how shared standards of expertise give other participants the incentive to improve their craft and succeed. For example, Briana,[3] a 25-year-old white woman from Utah, quickly became a top achiever of her Hogwarts house within *Hogwarts at Ravelry* and was promoted to the role of teacher within a few months of joining. Briana was also a pattern designer and seller, and she used these skills to test patterns for other *Hogwarts* members and to design a *Harry Potter*–inspired pattern for the group. As a teacher, she was tasked with creating assignments that helped students advance their knowledge of the *Harry Potter* universe while instilling important skills in less experienced members. Briana's "promotion" within the online affinity network was a signal of her rise in status within the community, and her role as teacher enabled her to curate important guides and resources for participants to learn from.

John and Hank Green, also known as the VlogBrothers, are the creators of the YouTube channel around which the *Nerdfighter* online affinity network coalesced (see the case study at the end of chapter 4). The brothers use their elite status to inspire their followers to help the world through community building and even donations to charity. The VlogBrothers' YouTube videos draw nearly 400,000 views on average, and they meld their interests in "everything nerdy" with an agenda they term "decreasing World Suck." As the VlogBrothers explain, "World Suck is exactly what World Suck sounds like. It's hard to quantify exactly, but, you know, it's like, the amount of suck in the world." As an example of decreasing World Suck, the VlogBrothers encouraged their fans to create a YouTube video about their favorite charity. In what followed, later termed Project for Awesome, fans uploaded hundreds of videos of their favorite charities and donated $870,000. These donations were then divided among 10 different causes that were voted on by *Nerdfighter* community members. The VlogBrothers used their elite status to rally the online affinity network around video production aimed at public good (see figure 3.5).

In both forums and interviews, *Sackboy Planet* members regularly refer to Sensei, a 25-year-old white male from the United States and a participant whom they hold in very high esteem (see the case study at

How To Be a Nerdfighter: A Vlogbrothers FAQ

vlogbrothers ☑

▶ Subscribe 2,866,345

1,826,063 views

+ Add to   ➤ Share   ••• More   👍 38,177   👎 422

Figure 3.5. Screen shot of the VlogBrothers video "How to Be a Nerdfighter: A Vlogbrothers FAQ."

the end of this chapter). In an interview, Sensei explained that some time ago he had an idol in the community before he achieved his own level of celebrity. "DarkMatter9 was my idol," he said. "The levels he made were so awesome that I wanted to know his secret. What was he able to do that I wasn't?" Idols, or elite affinity network participants, provide inspiration to community members as they learn to develop critical competencies in their craft. Sensei described DarkMatter9 as having a "secret," or set of skills that Sensei did not yet know but wanted to learn. Until Sensei got to know him better, DarkMatter9 stood as an "inspirational" symbol of achievement, "a huge motivator" on the road to improving himself as a designer.

As Ito (2012a) finds among high-status AMV creators, idols on *Sackboy Planet* rarely interact with the general public and instead stay closer to other high-status participants. "Celebrity status helped me reach more people and I could find those people I work well with," said DarkMatter9, a white male from the United States. "All the people I work with tend to be celebrities themselves . . . I've never had someone successfully solicit [level design] help from me through the fan sites . . . it became tiresome to be constantly helping." Although elites are less accessible to other community participants, their celebrity was produced, in part, by the content they shared with the community. For example, Sensei created an elaborate set of curated wikis and YouTube videos to teach others to manipulate logic for game design. Other celebrities devote a great deal of time and effort organizing major competitions in the community. On *Sackboy Planet*, elite participants earn their marks by setting the bar for valued skills and practices and by sharing valued content that the community appreciates. As a result, they create ideals that others in the affinity network aim to achieve.

Members of the *StarCraft II* affinity network (see the end of chapter 1) all know Day[9].[4] A former Pan-American *StarCraft* champion and the owner of the esports company Day[9]TV, the 25-year-old white Californian is a symbol writ large of achievement to *StarCraft II* players. Leagues such as the *War of the States* and the *North American Star League* are examples of national and international competitions in which players test their skills against some of the strongest competitors in the nation. Players such as Day[9] who compete in and win major esports competitions attain a level of celebrity among members of the *StarCraft II* affinity network. Day[9]'s elite status is based on his success as a competitive player and his instructive videos on how to play the game. Through his work as a commentator on the show *Day[9]TV*, he sees himself as an "educator" who shares strategy: "Solid play doesn't revolve around tricks, surprises, or hidden information, but very solid and strong [planning] and crisp execution." He parlays his status as an elite player and strategist to organize events and high-level partnerships, such as when Facebook developers hosted a tournament he was involved in (for an example of a *StarCraft II* tournament, see figure 3.6).

In the AMV affinity network (see the Animemusicvideos.org case study, this chapter) AbsoluteDestiny stands out as an accomplished elite who, like Sensei and Day[9], navigated the network's status system to achieve his social position and later found ways to give back. By posting frequently in the community and giving feedback to others before sharing his own first video, AbsoluteDestiny set the stage for people to give him a chance and help him move forward. As his craft improved, he started to win awards, began attending conventions in the United States, and started establishing himself as a high-status participant. The AMV

Figure 3.6. A *StarCraft II* tournament hall, Dreamhack 2011.
Image from Arthur Lee (https://www.flickr.com/photos/artr/6404108455).

community holds his work in high regard, and he uses his position to do important community organizing and management in the interest of other participants. For example, he helps out with design for the website, oversaw administration for the forums for a period, and serves as a judge for competitions at conventions. Our analysis of elites such as AbsoluteDestiny highlights the importance of status to expertise-oriented online affinity networks. Elites provide commonly recognized ideals of skill development and achievement that set the bar high for others to work to achieve. Elites also often serve important purposes within the community, such as curating high-quality informational content so others can learn how to improve their craft.

In this section we have documented how our cases comprise subcultures with various status systems that include their own established rules, requirements, expectations, and linguistic and dialogic standards. Network participants move across these systems as they seek status and recognition, such as when they push out their creations for the community to evaluate. These practices are also tied to formal markers of status, such as gamified currencies or badges. Elites establish ideals for skill development and set the bar high for others as they strive to achieve. High-status participants also engage in curatorial work to provide other participants with opportunities to learn and improve their craft.

Of note are the small numbers of young women elites in our cases. Many women in Ravelry and Wattpad "rose to the top," but these numbers were fewer in technically elite specialties. Among the exceptions—women players of *StarCraft II* and on *Sackboy Planet*, especially—some noted that there might have been some potential gendered barriers as they climbed the ranks. These findings are particularly notable given that we have actively sought out cases that value inclusivity, knowledge, and expertise. While it is challenging for women players to succeed in any competitive gaming culture, the *StarCraft* community is at the more positive end of the spectrum in its stance toward women. For example, one elite *Street Fighter* player quipped that sexual harassment is just part of the culture of fighting games, and if you removed that, "it's *StarCraft*" (Hamilton 2012). While we highlight the inclusive dimensions of online affinity networks, we recognize that it takes more than good intentions and a handful of positive exceptions to transform pervasive cultural hierarchies and social exclusions.

All online affinity networks navigate a complex balance between exclusionary and inclusive dynamics; they traffic in insider referents and mark status and achievement, but they must also recruit and retain new members to stay active. The online affinity networks in our study have particularly high standards for shared values, norms, and markers of quality; they also have well-developed ways of welcoming new members and inculcating the norms and standards of the core group. The networks we studied provide examples for how groups can avoid status systems that become unyielding barriers to participation. Online affinity networks that support connected learning maintain low barriers to entry by providing structures that teach subcultural capital to newcomers. In the next section, we describe how the groups we studied balance exclusivity and inclusivity, keeping barriers to entry low and guiding and leveling up new participants.

Leveling Up among Compartmental Intimates

Our cases provide examples of how the norms around earning subcultural capital are taught to new participants so that they can effectively engage with others, improve their craft, and achieve. We find that inclusive online affinity networks develop roles that are designed to welcome and mentor new members. These roles, which are embedded in an existing subculture and its status system, impart subcultural capital that less experienced members need to level up. They are also associated with the new members' development of compartmental intimates, affinity network–specific relationships that bond them to the shared purpose of the community and support them as they learn and grow.

Teachers, Mentors, and Moderators

In the previous section we described how the online affinity networks we studied boast a social architecture that regulates status within their communities. Here we describe how these thriving networks all have recognized roles for community members who support, guide, and mentor less experienced participants. In many of our cases, veteran participants organize activities that help those who are new to the scene gain subcultural capital. In this way, members who have achieved status and recognition can also contribute to the growth and inclusivity of the online affinity network.

One of the strongest examples of how high-status expert members welcome new members is from the *Hogwarts at Ravelry* case (see the end of chapter 4). Teachers are cornerstones of life at each of the houses and organize important lessons and activities. Teachers are typically appointed as a result of their successes as students in the community. For example, a course called "Bibliomagic" that was created by group leader Knitting-Principal,[5] a 43-year-old white woman from Idaho, required students to research and craft something representing the ancient Royal Library of Alexandria and the *Harry Potter* Durmstrang Institute. To complete these assignments, students needed to learn the Celtic ogham runic alphabet. For this lesson, KnittingPrincipal created links to online resources and encouraged students to report back on what they learned. She also defines the boundaries of appropriate topics. For example, she states in one post that "*Hogwarts at Ravelry* is completely, 100% non-political with regards to Muggle Elections." She points participants to other Ravelry groups that do allow political conversations, but she states firmly that she believes that "in an online community, it is far too easy for misunderstandings and hard feeling to occur. . . . I refuse to allow this place—this home—to become sullied by those kinds of disagreements."

Teachers at *Hogwarts* also design opportunities within the school structure to induct new participants into the culture and teach appropriate ways of engaging and learning before officially joining a *Hogwarts* house. New members are directed to the Visiting Wizards Hall, for people who are not yet sorted into houses and which provides a few basic projects to get the feel for creating knits as part of the community. These introductory-level products, termed "school supplies," include blanket squares that can be used to make Ron Weasley blankets, a wand, a wizarding pet, and a cauldron. Pattern suggestions are linked for each of these entry-level tasks. While new members are in this starter zone, teachers encourage them to participate in the formal classes. They are awarded points for participating in Visiting Wizards Hall and in the classes, and these points go toward each member's new house once they are officially sorted. Teachers also encourage new members to participate in forums specific to the house they hope to join. In this way, newbies can ask questions of more experienced members, receive socialization into the banter and role-playing standards of the community, and observe how others successfully participate in the group and during classes. Teachers, invited into their role by rising in status as *Hogwarts* participants, contribute by creating lessons, activities, and curated resources for participants to learn the lay of the land and improve their skills as knitters. Teachers also design and implement a space for new members to practice learning the ropes of the community and facilitate their full participation once sorted into the houses. These practices help new members develop relationships with their peers and higher-status participants, such as teachers, who impart subcultural capital.

Members of the Bollywood dance affinity network also inhabit important roles that help drive teaching and learning within their community (see the end of chapter 2 for the case study). Captains and lead dancers take on responsibility to support their team members. One leader, Neesha, who lives in California, described it as "basically like running a business." These leaders set up team goals, organize prop- and video-making activities, and provide their team members with advice on the use of digital tools such as GarageBand and video-production tools. One team leader, Jaya, from Illinois, used video as part of a rehearsal process for her team by recording their dances for later feedback and help. "I think recording was a very good tool because people could actually see what was needed to be improved," she explained. These leaders serve as organizers and support systems for day-to-day team activities and help to improve their members' skills in dance and, at times, even digital production.

Sackboy Planet members also ask experienced members to help newcomers to the level-design game learn the lay of the land (see the case study at the end of this chapter). For example, affinity network leaders identify players who are active and helpful to others to serve as moderators. Moderators typically pursue their work with gusto; being selected by the *Sackboy Planet* leaders to moderate is considered a flattering recognition of their budding fluency with community practices and procedures. One of the moderators' tasks is to welcome new members and guide them to resources aimed at socializing them into the community. New players are encouraged to post on a page for "Introductions" to share a bit about themselves and why they joined *Sackboy Planet*. Every introductory post is responded to within a matter of hours. Many responses to introductory posts are welcoming and identify resources that can help socialize new players into the community: "Hello and welcome to *Sackboy Planet*! This is the perfect place to you. To help you get started, I'll provide some links just for you. You might want to check out the Level Arena where you can share ideas you have for new levels to create. You can also ask others for help on your ideas and can receive advice about design." Players join *Sackboy Planet* for a variety of reasons, and moderators actively connect with new members to guide them to the resources that might best suit their interests, including specific directions and links to resources provided by other community members on how to improve their skills.

Roles such as moderators, teachers, and mentors are key components of a thriving and inclusive online affinity network, providing valuable learning resources and connection points between more and less experienced members, and defining the scope and tone of shared topics and activities. Just as with many traditional student-mentor relationships, these social relationships are specialized and often compartmentalized to the specific subject at hand. Yet they can be strong and often influential relationships in young people's lives because they can reorient a learning trajectory or identity. In much the same way that schoolchildren can be shocked to see a teacher out of context in a supermarket or other community setting, the relationships between mentors and mentees are both influential and context specific.

Community-Driven Supports

In the various communication channels of each of the online affinity networks, such as forums or chat rooms, network participants actively identify and reach out to those who need help, and at times enforce the standards of their network by warding off bullies who would detract from their learning community.

Although moderators on *Sackboy Planet* serve important roles as educators and welcomers to new participants, everyday members also work to identify low-status participants in need of help and to redirect problematic behavior. For example, when asked if nonmoderators ever step in and do something when they see bad behavior, PonyPal, a 17-year-old Latino from the United States, responded by explaining his own initiative during interaction with others in the forums: "I've never been a moderator or administrator or anything and I don't really care to. But I'm kind of like a non-moderator moderator. I tell people what I think or defuse situations. Or if I don't do it publicly I'll write them a private message." It is not only high-status elites, but also members of the broader community, who mediate conflict and explain to others what the expectations are for dialogue. When an affinity network has shared norms and values that all active participants buy into and support, online communication is responded to iteratively in a distributed way.

Everyday community members actively identify newcomers and reach out to them to provide support. For example, in the *Wrestling Boards* (see the end of chapter 1 for the case study), new members who need socialization are identified as "marks," which stands for someone who does not recognize that wrestling is choreographed. Part of the goal of the community is to educate new members who are marks and turn them into what they call "smarks," or those who are smart and educated about wrestling and the fandom more generally. Part of this socialization process includes learning how to provide feedback, help, and compliments on others' creative products. Jonathan, a white 16-year-old from the United Kingdom, describes how he interacts with his peers on the forum. "I give and get feedback often about what I do. I often help/mentor new members of the forum to the best of my ability. At the end of the day, we're all alike and we're like a family on The Wrestling Boards." Members of the community who participate in the fantasy wrestling federation are asked at the end of each week to rate the matches and give feedback, and the feedback is expected to meet certain quality standards.

Zach, one of the participants in the fantasy wrestling federation, describes his feedback for the writers: "I really look into [the fantasy wrestling federation] and try to help them improve it by writing reviews of their work so they can improve." In one response, a participant's feedback was far too brief: "Liked the show really good, can't wait for new show." In reaction, the poster replied: "Please answer every point I made. We want a good review not just a one sentence one. I even said so in the original post." As this example shows, reactions to participants' comments and posts pull others toward the community's feedback standards. In another example, a reviewer critiqued a misstep in using proper forms of English:

MAVEN: The lack of proper grammar is strong in these two. No wonder I had to do Heavy Jones' work for him last week. You're welcome by the way.

ZACH: I lol'd

MAVEN: @Zach As in it was funny or did I make grammatical errors myself? English is not my mother tongue so I try to keep on a look out for them.

ZACH: Nope, it was funny that you called him out because it had been bugging me.

Maven, as a nonnative speaker of English, corrects and edits others' work as a way to maintain the collective standard of grammar in writing. In this way, everyday members form relationships with others that have the effect of teaching subcultural capital.

The *Sackboy Planet* community also actively forms relationships with new members to socialize them into standards for participation. For example, earlier we described how participants are expected to share their work in certain ways on the forum; otherwise their work is ignored. Community members reach out to new participants to teach these standards of etiquette. The following is an excerpt from a forum post:

BLUEBELL: Hey guys I'm new to all of this, but if you could just spend 30 seconds of your time to click this link and subscribe to me, it means a lot.

RANGERGUY: Hi and welcome to *Sackboy Planet*! It's great to have you here, but here is a suggestion. Before asking people to subscribe to your youtube channel and play your level, maybe tell a tiny bit about yourself. What brought you to the site, your experience, etc. Most people here are nice and more than happy to help out. Look forward to seeing you around!

FLOWERPOWER: Welcome to *Sackboy Planet*. Lots of good information above. I agree with Rangerguy, let people get to know you first.

In this conversation between a new user and more experienced participants, members of the community provided guidance to BlueBell in the form of a corrective about appropriate ways to broadcast creative content.

In addition to providing ongoing guidance about community norms, participants also signal transgressive behaviors that inhibit respectful engagement. For example, members of the AMV affinity network (see case study at the end of this chapter) enforce appropriate means through which to share creative products. One editor recounted a time when a participant shared "cat turds" or low-quality work in the wrong way: "Just last night there was some guy on animemusicvideos.org who posted a new thread employing people to take a look at his video because it—and in the video's description, it was, like, bow to the God, this is the greatest thing ever . . . and everybody is just like, dude, shut up . . . have a little humility. And the thread just deteriorated." A community norm is that people share their work in ways that are not boastful and convey an openness to feedback and constructive criticism. "They may have potential to do stuff reasonably well," he noted, "except they squandered the potential because they don't listen to anybody who doesn't think their stuff is great." Network participants react to the tone of forum communications in ways that mark and stifle transgressions.

On *Sackboy Planet*, this takes the form of collectively identifying and policing "trolls." In one thread, members talked about a user who was using foul language and trying to take people away from the website:

FROG51: The troll who claimed to be a community member is some idiot who is swearing over and over and telling people to go to a different forum.

GOALIE1991: He's now posting this comment in every part of the forum. Someone please stop him.

BIGREADER: He's trying to steal people here to go to other places, and his actions are very irresponsible and he is spamming everyone. This is unforgivable behavior!

In this example, swearing and drawing attention away from the forums was identified as a flagrant violation of community standards. On *Sackboy Planet*, as in many online communities, attention from other members is a scarce resource. Both community elites and everyday members invoke the status systems within their online affinity network to identify newcomers in need of help and to ward off behaviors that do not meet their standards of etiquette. Next, we describe how participants reflect on the benefits of these relationships, or compartmental intimates, as they navigate their networks and strive to level up.

Peer Learning and Leveling Up

The online affinity networks we examined support a culture of peer learning, in which there is a give-and-take of knowledge and feedback. This can take the form of teacher-student–like relationships, "practice partners" who spar with one another in online games, or simply fans and fellow enthusiasts who geek out together on insider knowledge. The resulting relationships offer valuable information as well as emotional support from people who share the same passions, interests, and concerns. For example, Sensei, the highly regarded level designer introduced above in our discussion of elites, explained how close personal relationships on *Sackboy Planet* were key to his development. When he was new to playing *LittleBigPlanet 2* he spent six months trying to learn how to design on his own, but when he found *Sackboy Planet* and met other creators, his learning reached a new level. "I saw that people were putting out tutorials and saw what people were making and from there it just took off." Through this he found examples of people's work that created things he did not know "the editor was capable of doing." He was ecstatic, exploring and trying new things. "From there it just got a whole new level of depth." He was an active participant on the forum, connecting with other members by asking for help and also offering solutions to others' design questions. As he gained expertise, he was eventually rewarded by being asked to be a moderator. The relationships Sensei developed, which emerged from the moderators' shared design and troubleshooting activities, provided the groundwork for his elite status.

In another example, Nick, a 20-year-old Asian male from the United States and a participant in the *Wrestling Boards*, explained how his new friends in the network spurred his learning. For about 12 years before he joined the *Wrestling Boards*, Nick would casually watch wrestling with friends locally, enjoying the action but not really mastering the jargon or participating in story lines or in-depth analysis of the wrestlers. "Before [joining the *Wrestling Boards*] I did not used to go on to WWE sites, read WWE news/spoilers, or even knew any wrestling terms," Nick said. "I did not even know what a heel [villainous wrestler] or face [heroic wrestler] meant. I always used to refer them as the good guy and the bad guy." However, joining the forum "helped [him] a lot." As a consequence of his participation on the *Wrestling Boards*, Nick developed expertise in the vocabulary needed to write wrestling matches.

In addition to being a source of information, the relationships that youth formed in the online affinity networks we studied provided emotional support and bonded youth to the shared purpose of their community. For example, Earth, a 21-year-old from Illinois and a member of *Hogwarts at Ravelry* (see the end of chapter 4), explained that her friendships in the community create a safe environment. "It's an active group and even now, I still relate to them a lot," she explained. "We talk a lot and ask lots of questions in different threads about all sorts of things. It's a place I go where I feel safe to say what I want." The relationships that network participants develop can provide emotional support for challenges members face both in and outside of the community. For example, *Hogwarts at Ravelry* members encourage each other as they apply for jobs, finish homework for school, struggle with a child's illness, or even mourn the loss of a husband. Jen2291 explains:

> I love the social aspect. Since I don't get to talk to real live people very often . . . the groups are my coffee klatch and watercooler all rolled into one . . . it helps keep me sane to be able to talk with folks . . . and to have them understand my fondness for yarn is a huge bonus. I can joke, I can share my projects, and I can ask for sympathy if I've had a hard day . . . I can peruse projects at 3 A.M., dream of challenge ideas, and feel part of something larger than just me sitting here by myself.

Members of the online affinity networks we examined develop friendships that provide informational and emotional supports to not only develop skills needed for success but also persist as learners who can face challenges they encounter along the way. These friendships are specific to the activities of their communities, and as such are best understood as a unique form of compartmental intimates who are situated within online subcultures where they play and learn.

Conclusion: Bonds but Rarely Bridges

The online affinity networks we studied share vibrant subcultures with complex systems of status that establish important ideals, maintain order, and cultivate budding crafters, designers, and writers. By drawing out examples of elites from several cases, we described how these experts within online affinity networks provide inspirational guides to new participants as they level up within their communities. Each of these affinity networks has its own distinct rules, standards, etiquettes, and protocols for appropriate dialogue that are often unknown to outsiders and new entrants. Teachers and mentors, as well as everyday members of these online affinity networks, reach out to new members to teach the network-specific know-how needed to participate. These processes for teaching valued competencies, or subcultural capital, are embedded in the same status systems that create exclusive groups of elites. To maintain an inclusive environment, communities must offer opportunities for newcomers to be guided by participants recognized as experienced and of high status.

The status, reputation, and feedback systems of learning-oriented online affinity networks provide an architecture that fosters bonding and learning in a specialized interest. In interviews, members reflected on the profound impact that these friendships had on their capacity to dream big and achieve. They also described how they were able to power ahead despite major obstacles they faced as a result of the acts of caring their online friends provided one another. Online affinity networks provide access to social networks and subcultural capital that are not otherwise available to young people in their local context, and they can diversify a young person's network in profound and unpredictable ways. Finding others who share and celebrate their niche interests, passions, and identities can be a heady experience that fuels engagement and learning.

We have selected groups that have potential for connection to academic, civic, and career domains, though many of the subcultural and peer-learning dynamics are also common to other online affinity networks that have robust participation around any specialized area of interest. "Specialized and intentional" does not necessarily translate to "nice," however. Online affinity networks run the gamut from those that thrive on trash talk and aggression to others, like the ones we studied, that embrace a friendlier and more inclusive ethos (Gee and Hayes 2010). It is impossible to gauge how prevalent welcoming and friendly groups are in comparison to harsher ones. With the rise of movements such as #gamergate, online hate groups, and toxic fandoms, we cannot ignore the dark side of online affinity networks. While these groups were not the focus of our study, we can extrapolate from our study that maintaining community norms, whether nice or nasty, requires ongoing investment. Striving for inclusive and troll-free online affinity networks is an effort that requires collective investment and development.

Additionally, this chapter and our study focus on those who navigate status systems to level up, but the majority of participants in the online affinity networks we studied do not climb to the top of the status ladder as part of their participation. For example, some of the youth we interviewed preferred to primarily hang out socially with others online rather than link these friendships to their creation and learning activities. None of the youth we interviewed were less social participants (or lurkers), likely a consequence of our sampling methods through social channels within these networks. Lurkers can learn through consuming information and observing interactions on curated wikis or forum posts, but they are not involved in the status and reputation dynamics we describe in this chapter. These learners may be recognized for their skills and knowledge in other settings in their family or local community, but our study design does not give us insight into the practices of participants who do not actively contribute. What we do know is that online affinity networks like those in our study reach large audiences who find value in the forums, how-to's, and YouTube videos that they produce, and that young people are increasingly relying on these kinds of resources for learning (Ito et al. 2010). Members of the online affinity networks in this study recognize that full participation can be challenging for many people, and therefore they work to keep barriers to participation low and share resources openly online. The benefits of learning, recognition, and belonging we described clearly accrue most significantly to those who are active participants. Likely significant though more diffuse benefits we have not investigated accrue to those who are lurking and grazing through related online resources.

Despite the learning benefits that come with participation in the subcultures of expertise-oriented online affinity networks, we find that they impose limitations on the extent to which learners' skills may be translated into greater opportunity beyond their interest group. Just as members spoke about the fascinating cultural forms and day-to-day routines that are unique to their subcultures online, they also periodically joked that those outside of the online affinity network would have no clue what it is that they did there—let alone how the skills they developed could be bridged into educational achievement at school or even into career opportunities. This observation stands in contrast to what Small (2009) finds at child-care centers, where compartmental intimates form within an organization that shares ties to other institutions, including the state. The online affinity networks that we describe here share few connections of this kind. As we explore in the next chapter, this affects the extent to which youth can apply the skills they develop from leveling up online with other key spheres of their lives, such as family, school, and career.

Sackboy Planet

Matthew H. Rafalow

Imagine you are a creative genius at the helm of a control room, the puppet master to an adorable humanoid knit character capable of executing your vision for an entire video game—from the look of the setting, to the playable characters, to the dialogue, to the story that unfolds for anyone who plays the game you created.[1] This is the capstone experience of *LittleBigPlanet 2 (LBP2)*,[2] a puzzle-based and maker-oriented video game that was released by Media Molecule in January 2011 for the PlayStation 3 (see figure C.3.1a).

The game quickly gained popularity upon its release and garnered a major following in the United States and the United Kingdom. The main story follows a character named Sackboy as he tries to save his home world, Craftworld, from an evil interdimensional vacuum cleaner called the Negativitron. Gameplay operates similarly to side-scrolling action games; you control Sackboy and jump through obstacles and figure out puzzles until completing the level. Key features of the game include opportunities for players to craft levels and planets within the galaxy of Craftworld. Central to the design of the game are a number of digital tools that give players the means to create their own levels, animations, character art, and soundtracks (see figure C.3.1b for a screen shot of the level editor). Through use of these tools, players gain technical expertise, get practice in creativity and problem solving, and have numerous opportunities to collaborate and share their creations. This focus on production—the game's tagline is "Play, Create, Share"—is enabled through the game's careful scaffolding: The game fluidly guides players from the play of a traditional side-scrolling game to use of the level editor, teaching players how to use the tools as part of actual gameplay.

Players learn how to use the game controller to select and modify objects, place stickers, use power-ups, and, most important, navigate the physics-based world. This scaffolded approach couples entertainment

Figure C.3.1a. Learning how to create with a mind to gravity is a key aspect of level design. Screen shot of the *LBP2* level editor.

Figure C.3.1b. Screen shot of the *LBP2* level editor.

with production, minimizing barriers to the construction of unique levels that can be shared and played by others. One designer described the game as "a creative tool, which just allows you to make whatever you like, really. It's a whole toolkit of materials, of bits of electronics." This framing of the game as a platform for player creativity permeates the game's marketing materials and is expressed across all levels of the game's design, from the embedded design tools, to community features that enable sharing and feedback, to the structure of actual gameplay.

LittleBigPlanet 2 and its associated player-created design communities establish a shared purpose around creative production, feedback, and the development of technical expertise through their various community initiatives. One of these online communities, *Sackboy Planet*, has more than 1,000 active members (23,000 have registered since its launch several years ago). The audience is best described as predominantly "geeky" and male, though outliers exist beyond these categories in the broader community. As part of their shared purpose to support and educate others in design, *Sackboy Planet* members collectively produce and curate in-depth tutorials and informational YouTube videos for new learners. The community establishes a shared purpose through its designated sections of the forums, where users reciprocally provide assistance to others as they work through issues with their designs. Community members also organize huge contests around the production of creative game levels with particular themes and requirements. Players of a variety of skill levels submit their works in progress through stages of the contest process, receive feedback, improve their designs, and then share final products for review by expert designers in the community. Winners are celebrated for their hard work and generate a feeling of excitement; this process aids in the production of ideals for the rest of the community to aim for in their work.

Leaders of *Sackboy Planet* designed forums in ways that allow participants to easily share and receive feedback on their game design creations. The site includes a number of formal reputation-metric features in the form of post upvotes, reputation bars that reflect activity, badges for achievements, and displays of hearts or likes for particular level creations. Within the game itself, players can view various "top" charts for games across different categories, including by number of hearts/likes, trending levels, and hand-selected "picks" from the company that designed the *LittleBigPlanet* franchise, Media Molecule. The forums also cultivate informal means to evaluate the quality of others' works, including feedback-for-feedback threads where participants provide advice about the others' works in progress. Both quantified metrics and informal reputation mechanisms, such as peer-to-peer reviews and sharing, work hand in hand to elevate the high achievers in the level design community through time.

Learner Story

Gadget42, a 15-year-old white male from the United States and a *Sackboy Planet* participant, is a 10th grader with passions for theater, English literature, and gaming. He loves school and spends most of his time with other thespians practicing for upcoming theater productions. Although he describes himself as an average student, he is definitely "more of an English/history person." He does well in science, "but English and talking and stuff is more my personality."

When not at school, Gadget42 enjoys playing *LBP2* and hanging out on *Sackboy Planet*. A friend introduced him to the game a couple of years ago, and he was hooked immediately and began experimenting with the level editor. "I liked it right away. I would build little cars . . . it was fairly simple at first but when I started to try more advanced things it got more difficult." Once he began tackling harder design challenges, he searched the internet for help and stumbled upon *Sackboy Planet*, where he found tutorials and a kind community. "The people were friendly . . . we all have something in common, which is LittleBigPlanet." He posted questions about design to solicit guidance from more experienced members, and as he honed his skills, he began to regularly offer help to those who had questions just like he had had. For Gadget42, the *Sackboy Planet* community invigorated the potential of the game and magnified his interest in learning how to design levels among supportive peers.

Like other *Sackboy Planet* members I spoke with, Gadget42 finds connections between his own academically oriented interests and the types of design challenges he tackles in the game. In particular, his experience with English literature lends itself to level creation. As an English student, he writes lots of stories that help him brainstorm better level designs. "I learn to develop a story arc, which then I use for LittleBigPlanet to create the beginning, the middle, and the end of the story level I'm making. Currently I am writing and making a murder mystery point-and-click adventure game." For Gadget42, the skills he developed in school as a student of English literature have productive overlap with level design. To create a successful level, he mixes computer programming with story development to make a murder mystery game.

Sackboy Planet was also a place where Gadget42 made new friends who became fellow gamers and collaborators on design creations. After hanging out with other players in the forums and in the chat room, he began building closer friendships with people who challenged his design thinking. "It's nice seeing other people's views about the game." As far as his day-to-day activity in the forums, he spends most of his time hanging out with his friends online by talking about shared interests and helping them with design puzzles. "Most of the time I'm helping out friends. Trying to figure out the [design] logic for *LBP2* and story and gameplay and stuff like that." Often, he and his friends will play *LBP2* levels together or co-create new levels: "On *LBP2* we can have four people online in Create mode. We all create the story as we go. Sometimes we write it out before. One of us creates the gameplay and the other does the aesthetics of the level. We all decide if one part isn't good enough to be in it or if it needs a little work."

Gadget42 exemplifies connected learning at work through interest-driven, peer-supported, and academically relevant activities in *LBP2* and on *Sackboy Planet*. His interest in the game and his passion for English literature overlap in ways that make learning complex computer-programming and game-design skills much more fun. When he or his peers need help, they reach out through email, text, or video chat and assist each other. Sometimes they even design together by generating their own management style agreed upon by the group. They develop roles (i.e., writing, aesthetics, gameplay) and frequently run ideas and creations by each other to ensure high-quality designs. Gadget42 finds support online for his interest in the video game, and the level design skills he develops connect to a number of academic subjects.

Animemusicvideos.org

Mizuko Ito

The fan scene for Japanese animation (anime) is one of the most wired and active geek culture networks on the planet.[1] United by their love of the unique aesthetic of anime, long-running narratives, and diverse genres, fans tirelessly share news, commentary, and media in conventions all over the world, as well as through every conceivable online platform and medium. They were among the first groups to develop massive networks for digital image and video distribution, fan subtitling, and web forums, and they are active creators of fan art, comics, videos, and music (see figure C.3.2). Clay Shirky has described anime as a perfect example of content that supports "meganiches"—groups that are massive in scale but also very culturally specific (Shirky 2006).

Anime music videos (AMVs) are an example of such a meganiche. These are fan-created remixes of anime that span a wide range of genres, including parody, tributes to particular series or characters, or commentaries on the fandom itself. Most commonly, they involve remixing the content of a particular anime series to music of the fan's choosing. Because the AMV scene originated in the English-language online fandom for anime, this generally involves a fan's remixing Japanese anime content to a popular U.S.- or European-origin song. In other words, these videos are cultural mashups that localize Japanese content to referents local to overseas fans of anime. The practice of AMV making originated in the early 1980s among U.S. fans who created the first AMVs by editing VHS anime tapes. In the 1990s, in tandem with the spread of digital video editing, the practice gradually became widespread in the fandom. Today, AMVs are a well-established genre of fan production within the worldwide anime fandom and are shared online through video-sharing platforms as well as in fan conventions. Popular AMVs and AMV editors have fans and viewership in the hundreds of thousands, and AMV screenings are among the most popular events at anime conventions.

Figure C.3.2. Screen shot of creator profile on animemusicvideos.org.

Animemusicvideos.org (or what AMV creators fondly call "*the org*") was founded in 2000 by a group of fans as a place to upload and share AMVs. Before the founding of *the org*, editors had to maintain individual websites and video-hosting infrastructure. *The org* provided the first centralized location for creators to curate their profiles and videos and share with a growing audience. The site functioned as a center of gravity for a growing community of AMV editors, and it grew to include forums and profile pages where creators could curate their work, provide feedback, and share techniques and best practices. While the audience for AMVs is diverse and reaches most corners of the online anime fandom, AMV creators tend to skew male and have high educational attainment. In an informal survey my team fielded on *the org*, respondents were overwhelmingly white (81 percent) and predominantly from college-educated households. The male/female split was 62 percent / 38 percent. One fan I interviewed described AMV editors as "the professors" of the anime fandom, signaling the high degree of education and technical skills needed to hone the craft.

The design of the site is optimized for the specific needs of AMV creators and viewers, and it has been the subject of continuous evolution and redesign by the volunteer site operators. The site is sustained by this volunteer labor and by member contributions of content as well as dollars. Participants are continuously reminded to provide donations for site upkeep. As of 2016, the forums alone had more than 800,000 members. The site grew steadily from 2000 to 2005, but after YouTube launched in 2005, it has seen declining numbers of video uploads. As a variety of video-hosting options became available on the commercial internet, editors have moved to more accessible hosting sites, and viewers share these videos through a wide range of networks and platforms. As the distribution of AMVs has become highly decentralized, creators are more likely to share on YouTube. While *the org* continues to be a destination for learning about AMVs and connecting with other creators, it doesn't occupy as central a role in the scene as it did in its heyday.

Initially, the site centered on mechanisms for storing and sharing video and on providing an online forum for the community to coalesce. As the site expanded in the 2000s, it grew to include increasingly sophisticated mechanisms for providing reviews, running competitions, and developing status and reputation. The site encourages viewers of AMVs to rank the videos they have viewed, and these metrics are aggregated into rankings that surface the most popular videos. Competitions such as viewers' choice awards and other more specialized contests are another way of marking status and popularity of videos. Given the tremendous volume of AMVs being produced and uploaded, these ways of ranking, sorting, and marking quality work are critical for allowing people to gain access to the best work in the genres they are most interested in. The vast majority of AMVs in circulation are created by new editors who edit the most popular series together with mainstream pop music. As one experienced editor, XStylus[2], a 28-year-old white male, explains, "Now that practically anyone can make one, everyone does make one. It makes it supremely difficult for a new video of only good quality to stand out." More experienced members of the community describe how, in addition to these site-level ranking mechanisms, they rely heavily on their existing relationships for recommendations of new videos and for tips and advice.

Creators of videos also describe the importance of expert knowledge, feedback, support, and help that *the org* and the broader AMV community provide. Through the years, expert editors have written detailed FAQs and editing guides that are hosted in the forums, and new and aspiring editors are directed there first. The forums provide a space for people to ask questions, offer tips, provide recommendations, and seek responses on project ideas and rough cuts. In addition, the site provides a template for more structured feedback in detailed viewer-review forms. These kinds of reviews can be quite detailed, and the editor whose work is being reviewed has the option of publicizing the reviews as part of the information attached to his or her video on the site. The affinity network of AMV creators extends beyond *the org* as well, as they chat via Internet Relay Chat (IRC) and meet up at anime conventions around the country and the world. The most "elite" editors in the scene meet up annually at Anime Weekend Atlanta, which is the convention that boasts the most extensive AMV program in the world.

Learner Story

The story of one AMV creator, 18-year-old Gepetto,[3] illustrates some of the ways in which *the org* has supported connected learning for one youth. In high school, Gepetto was an avid fan of anime. Living in Brazil, he was dependent on peer-to-peer sharing of anime downloaded from the internet and other sources. On one CD of anime that a friend had burned for him, he found a small AMV clip. "Today I don't think much of it, but back then I was amazed at the idea that such a pretty little videoclip was made by a fan just like me . . . I put it on a loop and watched it several times in a row. . . . I left the computer on all night and downloaded a few AMVs. I liked them all, and began thinking 'what kind of video would I really want to see?'" His first step was to mess around with editing software on his own and make his first AMV. "It took about two and a half hours to make and was extremely horrible. But I loved it." At that time, he said, "I didn't know a video from a chicken," but he was an active fan and an avid fanfiction writer already, and he had a small group of anime fan friends at his school. He shared his AMV with his local friends, and one of them also decided to try his hand at it. Eventually Gepetto's quest for AMVs and his desire to create them led him to a range of online resources, including *the org*. "I get a lot of help at the animemusicvideos.org forums (a LOT of help) and at CreativeCOW (http://forums.creativecow.net). The doom9.org forums are also a great place for info on compression, but I'd say 98% of my troubles are solved at *the org*."

He went on to be a highly active member of *the org*, logging into the forums without fail every day. "I love the forums, I love the chats, I love answering questions and having mine answered in turn. I could spend 24 hours straight discussing AMVs without so much as a coffee break." He was also making a bid to be part of a large-scale collaborative editing project, which he saw as potentially a way of becoming "super strong and bulletproof." In other words, Gepetto was becoming a highly active and known member of the affinity network and building social capital, something that would be cemented through inclusion in a high-status project run by elite editors. Although he has been active online for years, *the org* is the first forum to which he has had this level of dedication.

Through his involvement in the AMV scene, Gepetto moved from someone who "didn't know a video from a chicken" to someone recognized as an expert both in the AMV scene and in his local community. In his 10th-grade art class, he was struggling to decide on a project, and then "it popped into my head, 'AMVs are art right?'" He put the two AMVs he had made onto a CD with some wallpapers he had made, handed them in, and received an A for the semester. His teacher encouraged him to make AMVs for the rest of his art credits for high school. Two of his friends heard about this and "managed to weasel into the 'project.' So now there's three people in Room 209 with twenty Dell Pentium 4 for 90 minutes every Friday." This group became a local, school-sponsored peer group that pushed his learning in digital arts beyond the simple editing of AMVs. The teacher was not an expert in digital media, and there were no digital arts programs at the school. But he encouraged Gepetto and provided critical space, resources, and validation. "The teacher didn't 'help' help, but he really stimulated me to go deeper into the technical part of AMVs. I wanted to make something that would _really_ impress him." The following year, his teacher invited Gepetto and his friend to teach a workshop for the ninth graders. Gepetto was just preparing for his third workshop at the time of our interview. He contrasts his status as a learner still seeking to break into the scene on *the org* to his status as an expert in his local community—"'something of a video expert' is anyone who knows the difference between a container and a codec in my community. So even though I know nothing, to them I am the Greater God of editing."

He was also in the process of applying for law school. He reflects on his aspirations:

> Believe it or not, I've been asked if I intended to make a career of AMVs by many older people who see my work. But I don't, and here's the reason: I'm inconstant. I only edit when I have the right mood and the right ideas. Whenever I force myself to do something in un-optimal conditions, I do it very very slowly. So, if I edited video for a job, there would be many times when I'd hate it, and I don't want to hate it. Another reason is keeping the freedom to choose exactly what footage I want to work with (shooting it myself in some cases) and not being handed a bunch of stuff to choose from.

He goes on to describe how he sees editing as a hobby and not a profession, and as something that he would like to be able to stop and return to as his time and interests wax and wane. Although Gepetto's journey through the anime fandom and the AMV scene did not lead directly to a career path, it is clear that the affinity network has shaped his identity, helped him acquire skills, and opened up unique opportunities for recognition in both his expert community and his local school-based one. Along the way he was supported not only by varied groups of peers locally and online, but by teachers who provided crucial points of translation and connection between his informal out-of-school learning and opportunities to excel at school. These linkages between specialized online resources and affinity networks and local support and opportunities for recognition represent the kind of ecology that young people require to realize connected learning.

4

Leveling Up

Connecting to Meaningful Opportunities

Lead Author: Crystle Martin

Introduction

Alex Giovanni, a 15-year-old white high school student from Florida, grew up in what he called a "video game family." "I was extremely lucky as a kid to have a family that was interested in gaming and that considered it a decent pastime," Alex told us (see the *StarCraft II* case study at the end of chapter 1). Not only did Alex have two siblings and a father who would play video games, but they would do so together as a regular family activity. On a typical day, they would first do their homework after school ended about 3:30 P.M. The whole family would eat dinner at 6 P.M. and played video games from 7 P.M. to 8 P.M. Saturdays were "big days," as his father and siblings would play through the evenings with him. While his mother was not interested in gaming, she was supportive of her boys. "She was always organizing the LAN parties, and getting the food and stuff like that," Alex recalled.

His brother, 10 years older than Alex and now owner of a software company, was particularly influential in nurturing Alex's gaming expertise. When they were growing up, Alex looked up to his brother in everything he did—*StarCraft*, anime, and other games. Because of this early exposure, Alex picked up *StarCraft* when he was just seven years old. He writes in a reflective blog post: "Through this exposure to my brother's friends [through LAN parties], many of whom were close to ten years older than me, I learned how to be competitive in a world far above my age. I found myself attempting to improve my vocabulary to sound like them, creating extensive biographies of characters to appear as engaged as they were, and adapting to the flow of success and failure as they had."

As Alex grew older, his gaming network shifted toward friends who were part of a high-achieving International Baccalaureate program at his high school. They played video games as well as *Magic the Gathering* and chess. Within the group, he found a friend who was interested in robotics, and they both participated in a robotics club known as Exploding Bacon Robotics. Unlike most gamers in his school, his group treats games "competitively and seriously." For them, *StarCraft* functions much like chess for earlier generations, straddling academics and competitive play. Inspired by the *Collegiate Starleague*, his peer group helped start the *High School Starleague*, a national league that includes hundreds of teams across the country. He also formed a club with his *StarCraft* friends, Meeting of the Minds, "dedicated to the principle of identifying problems and creating practical solutions." They developed a plan to run a one-day event dedicated to educational reform. Although they were not successful in getting their school to sponsor this event, his *StarCraft* friends rallying in support of his plan left a lasting impression. "My group of *StarCraft* friends changed from simply a group for gameplay to a community in which my friendships integrated into my school life, in restoring my passion for education, as well as my civic life."

For Alex, the social bonds, skills, and civic dispositions that he developed through his involvement in *StarCraft* became a foundation for academic achievement, community organizing, and activism. He sees the hardworking, intellectual, competitive orientation of his peers as integral to how they approach both academics and gaming. Further, the experiences he had organizing in the *StarCraft* community propelled him to civic action. These connections to achievement and civic action contrast with how gaming is commonly depicted, as an anti-intellectual and antisocial pastime that does not have a place in the culture of schooling. Young people such as Alex, who create new and unconventional connections among their online affinity networks, school, and civic life, are more the exception than the rule.

Most of the activities we observed and the young people we spoke to were focused on the bonding and status building that were internal to the online affinity network rather than on building connections outward. However, we did see examples of groups and individuals, like Alex, connecting the relationships and skills developed in their online affinity networks to academic, civic, and career opportunity. Approximately a third of those we interviewed saw some benefit to their participation in their online affinity networks for career, academics, and civics. Roughly one-sixth of those we interviewed made *direct* connections to opportunities outside of the online affinity network, as Alex did. Given that our interviewees are already heavily skewed toward those most likely to make these connections, we recognize that cases such as Alex's are rare. This chapter chronicles these exceptional examples of how learning in online affinity networks can connect to pathways that lead to opportunity. After first framing how we understand learning across settings, we describe how young people connect their online affinity networks to academic, career, and civic opportunity.

Connecting Learning across Settings

In the online affinity networks we studied, young people are developing specialized knowledge, skills, and relationships that could serve them in their academic, civic, and career pursuits. As described in the prior chapters, however, a large part of the appeal to youth of even our selective group of online affinity networks lies in their disconnection from the mundane realities of schoolwork and from the scrutiny of their peers in their local community. When interests are stigmatized or niche, the online affinity networks become havens of people who "get it," in which young people can debate esoteric topics with a specialized lingo incomprehensible to outsiders. This bonding around niche interests takes on the quality of "compartmentalized intimates" (Small 2009), in which relationships are both bonded and bounded. These qualities of online affinity networks can be challenging to parlay into the knowledge and opportunities that are recognized in the adult world, such as academic subjects, economic opportunity, and civic involvement. The disconnect between the culture of the online affinity network and the culture of schooling and career is likely even stronger in groups that are less focused on creative production and expertise. When these connections *are* made, however, they are powerful because they are anchored in deeply held interests and affinities. How are these connections forged, and what conditions support this connection building?

The problem of how learning connects across settings is a long-standing concern of the learning sciences. Traditionally, this has been framed as a question of how classroom learning "transfers" to other settings. Transferring learning from one setting to another setting turns out to be a complicated task; it is not a simple matter of acquiring generalized knowledge, skills, and frameworks that apply to other life settings. Indeed, a 2012 National Academies report on "deeper learning" concluded that "over a century of research on transfer has yielded little evidence that teaching can develop general cognitive competencies that are transferable to any new discipline, problem or context, in or out-of-school" (Pellegrino and Hilton 2012). This consensus reflects decades of sociocultural learning research that critiques the ways in which classroom learning is cut off from meaningful social practice and student interests (Lave 1988; Lemke 1990; Varenne and McDermott 1999). Unlike everyday learning, or "on the job" learning in work settings (Hutchins 1994; Lave 2011; Rose 2014), sequestered classroom learning presumes that learning from a more controlled setting can transfer to a more dynamic and variable set of contexts. Paulo Freire ([1970] 2000) has critiqued this approach as a faulty "banking" model of education that assumes learners can "save up" knowledge in school and "cash in" later in life.

A lack of connections between the classroom and the wider world is particularly harmful for students whose interests and identities do not align with the dominant culture of schooling. Progressive educators have considered ways in which in-school and out-of-school learning could more productively be knit together for children and youth who are not from the dominant culture (Freire [1970] 2000; Gutstein 2012; Hull and Shultz 2002; Nasir and Hand 2008). For example, Kris Gutiérrez and Barbara Rogoff (2003) have suggested that "repertoires of practice" from students' home culture can be connected to school. The movement for culturally relevant pedagogy (e.g., González, Moll, and Amanti 2005) is another example of working across the boundary between school and home cultures. A growing body of research suggests that successful transfer requires connections and conversion points between a learner's in-school and out-of-school settings (Beach 1999; Bransford and Schwartz 2001; Engestrom 1996). Taking this socially situated perspective, Beach has suggested "a reconceptualization of transfer as consequential transition among social activities" (1999:104). He goes on to specify that "a change in relation can occur through a change in the individual, the activity, or both. Transitions are consequential when they are consciously reflected on, often struggled with, and the eventual outcome changes one's sense of self and social positioning" (1999:114). In other words, successful "transfer" is not determined purely by what is in the head of an individual and requires connections and transitions across disparate cultural referents, social practices, and institutions.

We draw from Beach's reconceptualization of transfer as a dynamic relation among individuals, activities, and settings, but we put more emphasis on connections than on transitions. In our observations and interviews with young people, we searched for "pathways," "transitions," and "trajectories," but these linear narratives were elusive. As described in chapter 1, we see learning and interest development as less a transition from one state to another and more a process of network building. The problem of supporting in- and out-of-school linkages rests on network diversification and cultural translation. Do young people have friends, parents, teachers, and mentors who help broker and translate across this divide? Do they have cultural referents and repertoires of practice that link in-school and out-of-school settings? While tackling the shared problem of learning across settings, we invert the long-standing question of transfer by focusing on the informal learning setting rather than on the classroom setting. We call attention to the learning in online affinity networks, and we ask how educators can connect that learning for advancement in academic, civic, and career-relevant contexts. Young people are now less reliant on educators for content expertise because of the growing abundance of information and affinity networks they can find online. As young people connect to sources of knowledge and expertise in their informal contexts, however, the need for brokers to connect in- and out-of-school learning grows. How can educators, parents, mentors, and young people themselves find ways to connect to, recognize, and acknowledge the learning that young people are already pursuing in their affinity networks?

Just as educational researchers have found it challenging to support and document transfer between classroom learning and the world at large, young people, parents, and educators in our studies have also struggled to see the relevance of informal, affinity-based learning for school, civics, and career. As noted throughout this book, young people's online affinity networks are often wrapped around unique and esoteric subcultures with their own status economies and what Arjun Appadurai (1988) has described as "regimes of value." Like other anthropologists who have analyzed cross-cultural encounters (Comaroff and Comaroff 2009; Myers 2002), he considers moments of contact and conversion between different systems of value and exchange. When a tourist buys a piece of folk art, for example, the value of that object is converted from the regime of the local culture to that of the visitor via a broker. In a similar fashion, the social and cultural capital that young people gain in their online affinity networks is not commensurate with the regimes of value of schooling, workplace, and civic life, and it needs to be converted and translated by a broker, whether that is through an organizational practice, parent, educator, or the young person himself or herself.

In the case of electronic games, digital arts, and pop cultural fandoms, this need is particularly acute because of the lack of institutionalized brokers and shared intergenerational referents. The lack of supports for these emerging interest areas contrasts to, for example, music or athletics, which span multiple generations and have strong institutional relationships that link learning and achievement across home, school, and community organizations. The interests are culturally valued, and parents and educators recognize how they develop qualities such as discipline, teamwork, health, and problem solving. Schools and universities have well-established mechanisms to convert out-of-school learning in these areas to status within the academic establishment. This can take the form of school-sponsored extracurriculars, résumé building, arts and athletic scholarships, and recommendations. It is only recently that schools and universities have been developing scholarships, portfolios, student clubs, and other forms of recognition for areas such as esports, digital arts, and online video. Our work is part of a small but growing cadre of scholarship that is surfacing the civically and academically rewarding dimensions of fandom and gaming (e.g., Black 2008; De Kosnik 2016; Gee and Hayes 2010; Ito et al. 2015; Jenkins et al. 2016; Martin 2014; Squire 2004; Steinkuehler 2007). We return to some of these emerging opportunity areas for parents and educators in the concluding chapter, "Moving Forward: Connections to Practice and Design." The remainder of this chapter is devoted to the connection building that we observed in our case studies, in which young people forged linkages between the learning in their online affinity networks and academic, civic, and career-relevant settings.

Connecting Interests to Achievement and Opportunities

Academics

Young people are developing a wide range of academically relevant skills and knowledge in online affinity networks. These include general competencies such as problem solving, collaboration, experimentation, and traditional and multimedia literacy, as well as more domain-specific content and skills such as coding, video editing, mathematical inquiry, foreign languages, and scientific knowledge. Many young people, however, do not see the relevance of their out-of-school interests for academic learning. For example, Crayo, a white 19-year-old from Northern England, describes what he has learned and what he gets from his experience on the *Wrestling Boards* (see the case study in chapter 1): "Fun, that's all really. The experiences I have learned are pretty much all online experienced which I guess has helped me keep in the know with the online phases (memes etc), but that's all." Tim Young,[1] a 21-year-old Asian college student from Southern California and, like Alex, a *Star-Craft* participant, has similar feelings about the learning that takes place for pro-gamers: "It's very weird, because it's very, like, meta-benefits. Being a pro-gamer, the skills you get as being a pro-gamer—isn't really something you can apply to real life." Even fanfiction writers (see the case study 1D on Wattpad at the end of chapter 2), who are developing writing skills and interests that seem directly relevant to school, often do not see the connection. Katie, a 15-year-old white teen from Australia, says of her writing on Wattpad that "it's not writing writing," like the kind she does in school. Not surprisingly, many young people, particularly if they have an unfavorable view of classroom learning, are invested in keeping their recreational interests sequestered from school and untainted by academics. The examples we describe in this section, and in the chapter more generally, are from young people who have bucked this dominant tendency.

The *Wrestling Boards* and One Direction (1D) case studies offer clear examples of young people developing literacies that are relevant to school. It is not uncommon in these networks to find young writers such as Maria, a 17-year-old Asian college student from the Philippines, who developed an interest and skills in writing after becoming involved in an online fandom for professional wrestling. Her experience with writing for the *Wrestling Boards*' fantasy wrestling federation made her "realize that I love writing." Role-playing forums such as the *Wrestling Boards* and online publishing platforms such as Wattpad are full of teens writing hundreds of pages of fanfiction inspired by their favorite characters and narratives, not to mention the millions of youth who read their work. Although many of these youth hide these activities from teachers and parents and might describe their writing as "not real reading or writing" in the school sense, it is clear that they are picking up school-relevant skills (Black 2008). Some, like Maria, may see their fan writing as directly tied to their decision to pursue writing in school and career. Sandra, a 15-year-old Asian high school student from Malaysia and a participant in the One Direction fanfiction affinity network, also describes her online writing as tied to her school achievement. "Wattpad certainly helped me improve my writing in school. I now get good marks for writing essays. . . . Before wattpad, my writing wasn't as good. . . . For personal development, I guess I got more self-confidence in me." Abigail, a 13-year-old white teen from Toronto, Canada, was able to get into a competitive creative writing program based on the writing skill she developed through her Wattpad experience.

Many of the online affinity networks also support the development of skills that are relevant to academic subjects as a side effect of participation. For example, Leo, a 16-year-old white teen from Brazil, used his participation in the *Wrestling Boards* as a way to improve and practice English, his second language. Researchers studying *StarCraft II* have documented gains in attention and cognition (Hotz 2012; Thompson et al. 2013), and we have also observed the complex problem solving and mathematical thinking involved in the game. Our observations of *StarCraft II* forums have yielded intriguing examples of collective mathematical problem solving. For example, players puzzled on the forums over a unique strategy deployed by one professional player, who was able to move his units through the activation radius of a "widow mine." Players submitted a variety of theories, illustrated through diagrams and screen shots (as seen in figure 4.1). Many of these included geometry-based mathematical thinking, such as the formula that a player named

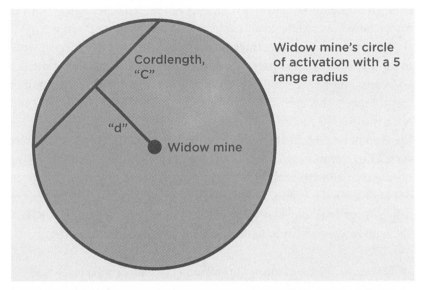

Figure 4.1. Graphical representation of Lone's math to explain life's strategy, reproduced based on the original diagram on TeamLiquid.net.

Lone posted on the *StarCraft II* player community message boards (Team Liquid 2013a).

> I based my calculations on chord lengths using the following formula:
> Chord Length = C = 2sqrt((r^2) − (d^2))
> I then solved for d, getting:
> d = sqrt((r^2) − (C/2)^2),
> Which we can plug r = 5 into, so my final formula became:
> d = sqrt(25 − (C/2)^2),
> Where:
> d = distance to Mine at closest point on chord (AKA Effective Radius)
> C = unit speed*1.5.

The importance of the chord length is that if a target moves within the radius of the widow mine in 1.5 seconds or less, the widow mine has enough time to target but not fire (C = unit speed times 1.5). This strategy helps players decide when they are getting too close, as well as providing guidance on getting in and out fast enough. Through this collective problem solving, players deployed their mathematical skills to understand how to effectively avoid setting off the mine (Young 2013).

We also saw similar geometry-based mathematical thinking at work in Ravelry.com when knitters developed patterns and calculated stitches and yarn lengths (see the case study *Hogwarts at Ravelry* at the end of this chapter). This is math with a purpose, and it often entails trial and error in situ. The math used by participants in Ravelry is more complex than might be evident at first blush; calculations are adapted as variables such as size of the yarn, measurements of the garment, and size of the needle change with each new piece. Amy, a white 17-year-old pattern designer from Colorado, uses math both in figuring out the designs of her own patterns and in helping others. Amy works with another Raveler who is worried her stitch count is off compared to the pattern:

> RAVELER: The directions say to knit until there are 44 stitches—which the sleeve will then pick up. However, when I followed the directions and knit 3" into the arm hole, I only had 13 stitches. not 15. So if I did the 44 stitches as instructed, it would be too long. My swatch is 15 stitches/3"
>
> AMY: I suggest doing the 44 stitches. Keep in mind, there is plenty of space in the underarms because of the decrease in stitches. Extra stitches there will be fine.

In this example, the Raveler is wondering which of the units to attend to, given that they are contradictory: the number of stitches in the pattern (44), or the length (3 inches). Amy, given her experience with knitting patterns, knows that the unit of stitches here is more important for the overall product than the unit of inches, and advises the Raveler accordingly. In other words, Amy knows that the mathematics of knitting can be inconsistent, unlike the length of the widow mine chord calculated above, and has enough experience with completed projects to predict what should be given priority. She helps a second Raveler who is worried that the arm sleeves will not be large enough for her:

> RAVELER: I'm excited to start this—it is beautiful! But I'm worried about the sleeve size. I want more room for my arms and am looking for an upper circumference of 16.5–17". Advice on which size I should pick?

AMY: This author tends to have large sleeve sizes—so that helps. It looks like a size 8 (which is 46" bust) should work for you. I've divided the number of stitches in the upper arm over the number of stitches per inch, though you should check your gauge. There are two parts—the stockinette part and the slipped-stitch part. The stockinette gauge is looser, something like 25 sts to 4"/10cm, not 26 sts to 4"/10cm like the slipped-stitch pattern. So when you make the front, you need to calculate the stitches and then divide that number by the 26 sts to 4"/10cm gauge. But the stockinette uses the other gauge.

In this example, Amy knows something about the underlying mathematical pattern: that the author has a tendency toward larger sleeve sizes. As a result, only certain adjustments to the pattern are necessary to achieve the Raveler's goal of wider sleeves, although the calculations are further complicated by the fact that different stitches produce different stitch-per-inch units. Amy makes some of the mathematical adjustments for the Ravelers, and then she advises them on how to adjust to their own idiosyncratic stitch-per-inch ratio. In short, to support other Ravelers, Amy needs to understand the underlying mathematical concepts.

Alissa, a 31-year-old white woman from Boston, explains how she learned to work with patterns since her early days of knitting: "I've never written a pattern but I have altered a few. Mostly through experimentation and a little math to get the calculations right . . . but mostly a lot of old fashion experimentation :)." Exhibiting a similar pragmatic approach, Holly, a white Raveler in her mid-30s from Maine, describes how she learned to calculate the yardage of her yarn. "The simplest way to do it is you take whatever's left over of the skein, and wrap it around your arm, and measure how much yarn one wrap is. And then wrap whatever you have left over from the skein, figure out how much that is and then subtract it from whatever your ball totals . . . if your skein is . . . four-hundred yards, and one wrap is one yard, and you wrap it ten times, then subtract ten yards and your project was 390."

Jen2291,[2] a 49-year-old white woman from Arizona, believes that seeing the wide range of projects on Ravelry pushed her math skills to new levels when she was first learning. "I was master of geometry—squares, circles, etc. (and you can make a lot of things with those shapes!) but it wasn't until I saw those other projects that I realized people make

EVERYthing out of yarn." Mary, a 21-year-old white Raveler from Ontario, Canada, reflects on her early knitting years: "I think the repetitive counting—stitches, pattern repeats—helps in other areas of life, simply because it exercises the math muscle." Andie, a 24-year-old Mexican American living in California, also notes how knitting "has helped keep my basic math skills sharp." The mathematical thinking of gamers and Ravelers is reminiscent of research conducted by Jean Lave on mathematics in settings such as shopping (1988) and tailoring (2011). She argues that *both* "applied" math and school math are context specific—"complexly imbricated in social, cultural, and historical relations" (2011:143). Rather than privilege school math and focus on transferability across settings, she suggests that we ask "what holds them together and interconnects what goes on in one with another" (2011:143)?

These examples of mathematical thinking are evidence of weaving and connection building between skills and activities in online affinity networks and school and other settings. We noted this same dynamic in other online affinity networks. Gadget42, a 15-year-old white male from the United States, is passionate about level creation in *LittleBig-Planet 2 (LBP2)* and about English literature (the case study *Sackboy Planet* appears at the end of chapter 3). He describes how he drew from his interest in English literature to develop story arcs for his *LBP2* levels, and conversely how his work in *LBP2* inspires his writing. "I learn to develop a story arc, which then I use for *LittleBigPlanet* to create the beginning, the middle, and the end of the story level I'm making. Currently I am writing and making a murder mystery point-and-click adventure game." Akash, a college student from Northern California, also drew connections between his engagement in collegiate Bollywood dance (see the end of chapter 2 for the case study) and his major in mechanical engineering. Akash used skills that he developed in his mechanical engineering training to build props and create short films that introduce his team's performances. He also designed and fabricated a tank for a military-themed dance number, which gave his team prestige in the competition circuit: "We actually get judged for what props we bring out and how we use them. . . . I designed and built the whole thing myself." The tank was an engineering challenge, because it needed to be "light enough to drag out on the stage and then immediately drag back off stage and still support all the choreo that they're doing inside."

When a young person is able to advocate for his or her interests in a school context and has the support of a teacher, both the student and the school setting can be enriched. For example, Gepetto, an 18-year-old from Brazil, was in high school when he began creating AMVs (see the Animemusicvideos.org case study at the end of chapter 3). He describes how he kept "forgetting" to get his sketchbook for art class, and when a new teacher took over, Gepetto submitted some AMVs instead and got an A for the term. His teacher "was very interested in having a student that did something so different, and asked me if I wanted to make an AMV at school for my arts grades, being dismissed of all other arts classes activities for it." Upon hearing about the deal Gepetto had struck, two of his friends also petitioned the teacher to be able to do a digital-arts project for art class, and they were able to form a small group that worked at the computers during art time. The teacher was not an expert himself, but Gepetto describes how he "didn't 'help' help, but he really stimulated me to go deeper into the technical part of AMVs. I wanted to make something that would *really* impress him." Eventually, this same teacher invited Gepetto and one of his friends to give a workshop to the younger students on video editing.

In other examples, too, of young people connecting their online affinity network activities to school achievement, we saw a caring adult—a family member or a teacher—helping by recognizing the value of the activity and brokering connections. Maria, the Philippine college student introduced earlier in this chapter, was able to connect her WWE writing to school because of a teacher whom she confided in and who encouraged her to write for the school newspaper. This same teacher mentored Maria in her decision to apply to a medical scholarship program. She chose to pursue a degree in the medical field, where she could use her strong writing and grammar skills for technical writing, and then to pursue creative writing as a second degree. One Direction fans were generally reluctant to share their fan activities on Wattpad with parents and teachers, but Sandra, the 15-year-old from Malaysia, did confide in her parents. Though they did not read her fanfiction, they supported her interest in it. She describes how this parental support helped her see the relevance of her fan writing for school. The gamers in our studies who drew connections between their interests and school also had parents who were supportive of their gaming. Alex's family was unusually supportive of his *StarCraft* activities, as we describe in the introduction to this chapter, but other gamers also described familial support. Gadget42, the 15-year-old level designer who is creating a murder mystery game, described how his father was fine with the amount of time he spent with *LBP2*. These examples suggest that with more parental and educator support, many more young people would be mining the academic relevance of their pursuits in their online affinity networks.

Civics

Online affinity networks can be a gateway to civic engagement for young people. As described in the prior two chapters, an important aspect of participation involves community organizing, collaboration, and orchestration of social networks. When young people become involved in the organization and leadership of online affinity networks, they can develop sophisticated civic and organizational skills, even when the group is not focused on civic and political issues per se. An analysis of two large panel studies of U.S. youth found a strong relationship between nonpolitical online interest-driven activity and civic and political engagement (Kahne, et al. 2013). Whether they are *StarCraft* players organizing tournaments, *LBP2* designers running a contest, or WWE and *Harry Potter* fans managing a message board, young people are gaining experience in developing community values and practices, navigating political tensions, and collaborating with peers. In addition to this common focus on community organizing, some online affinity networks we observed engage in civic and political action as the key focus. Others participated in acts of charity and civic engagement as a secondary practice, or in specific moments when the opportunity arose. We describe examples of more explicit civic and political action in this section.

In other work, we have studied and analyzed youth networks that are held together by a set of affinities and interests that are explicitly civic and political in nature. In collaboration with the Media, Activism, and Participatory Politics (MAPP) project led by Henry Jenkins (Jenkins et al. 2016), we analyzed examples such as the DREAM Activists, Invisible Children, teen reporters for Youth Radio, and *Harry Potter* fans mobilizing for social good in the Harry Potter Alliance. Drawing from the connected learning model (Ito et al. 2013), we described how these groups support "connected civics." Connected civics involves young people pursuing civic activities that are peer supported and rooted in their personal interests and identities (Ito et al. 2015). The case of *Nerdfighters*, represented in this book (see the case study at the end of this chapter), comes from the MAPP body of case studies and represents a group in which the core focus of "decreasing World Suck" is civic in nature. For example, the Project for Awesome is an organized annual event for which *Nerdfighters* create videos in support of their favorite charity or nonprofit. After the first year, in which they tried to take over the front page of YouTube with their videos, *Nerdfighters* partnered with YouTube. About a quarter of all *Nerdfighters* participated in Project for Awesome in 2013, when *Nerdfighters* uploaded hundreds of videos and more than 24,000 people donated to the *Nerdfighters* charity. They collected $870,000 in donations and divided them among the 10 causes whose videos received the most votes from the community.

For the majority of the other cases in the Leveling Up study, civic engagement was either a secondary or periodic activity. Apart from *Nerdfighters*, *Hogwarts at Ravelry* (see the case study at the end of this chapter) practices the most consistent set of civic and charitable activities. When *Hogwarts at Ravelry* members submit crafted items to the group's classes and challenges, members are awarded extra points if the item was crafted for a charity. The group also developed a special award and badge, the St. Mungo Award, named after the hospital in the *Harry Potter* series. This award honors members who perform charitable work, and it was the second award that the group created after the House Cup competition, which is the main competition for Ravelers. *Hogwarts at Ravelry* went on to organize a series of challenges in which different charities were picked each month and then Ravelers would make items for them. These charitable efforts included collecting knitted items such as mittens for orphans in Canada, hats for neonatal intensive care unit (NICU) babies or cancer centers, small mice to raise money for the Alzheimer's Society, and even vests for penguin victims of an oil spill. Pilots, a 21-year-old from Portland, Oregon, describes how she started knitting for charity: "My first project coming back [to knitting] was baby hats for the NICU. My first hats were disastrous! It's a project that's always been near to my heart though and even now I still really enjoy knitting for babies (I've expanded beyond the NICU)."

Although *Hogwarts at Ravelry* is exceptional in its sustained attention to charity, it is not uncommon for fan and gaming communities to mobilize periodically for charitable causes. Anime fans organized fundraisers in the wake of the 2011 tsunami and nuclear disaster in Japan (Yune 2011). In 2008, millions of Korean youth took to the streets to protest government policy, particularly its lack of attention to beef imports during the panic over mad cow disease. A subset of these teens included Korean boyband fans protesting in order to "protect their boys" from mad cow disease (HyeRyoung Ok, personal communication, 2009). In the *StarCraft II* community, Team Liquid, a professional *StarCraft* team, hosted a charity livestream of its matches called "StarCraft without Borders" to raise funds for Doctors without Borders. These are all examples of young people activating their existing affinity network for civic and charitable purposes that resonate with their collective values.

In addition to these charitable activities, we also saw online affinity networks mobilize for political or social causes that grew out of their self-interests, identities, and self-expression. We saw Ravelry take a political turn in the summer of 2012 after it organized the Ravelympics, an Olympics-themed knit-along that mobilized more than 12,000 Ravelers. The U.S. Olympic Committee (USOC) issued a cease and desist order that included the following statement: "The USOC is responsible for preserving the Olympic Movement and its ideals within the United States. Part of that responsibility is to ensure that Olympic trademarks, imagery and terminology are protected and given the appropriate respect. We believe using the name 'Ravelympics' for a competition that involves an afghan marathon, scarf hockey, and sweater triathlon, among others, tends to denigrate the true nature of the Olympic Games. In a sense, it is disrespectful to our country's finest athletes and fails to recognize or appreciate their hard work." Ravelry members swiftly mobilized to denounce the language and demands of the USOC. They contacted local radio and news stations, blogged, and used social media to criticize the USOC and build support. One Raveler staged a "knit-in" at the USOC headquarters, and members discussed how to carry out an economic boycott of the many sponsors of the U.S. Olympic teams. Their fast and passionate outcry garnered a quick response from the USOC, and within 24 hours it issued two apologies, stating that the USOC sincerely regretted "the use of insensitive terms in relation to the actions of a group that was clearly not intending to denigrate or disrespect the Olympic Movement. We hope you'll accept this apology and continue to support the Olympic Games." Although the USOC did not back down from the cease and desist demand, the apology quelled most of the fury, and the knit-along continued under the new name of the Ravellenic Games. More than 12,000 Ravelers participated by submitting 46,000 projects, and more than 3,000 of those projects were donated to charities (Pfister 2014).

An example of an affinity network supporting a social cause comes from the Bollywood dance case study (see the end of chapter 2). Shresthova (n.d.) describes the story of one dancer, Yuri Doolan,[3] and how he used collegiate dance competitions as a stage to elevate awareness of LGBTQ issues in his community. He conceived of a dance for his team at Northwestern University that centered on a young Indian American man's coming-out story. The story mirrored some of his own struggles "negotiating issues of sexuality while being Asian American or second generation American." He was nervous when first sharing his ideas with his team and then during the first performance. But in both cases the community warmly embraced his message. "I really couldn't have imagined a better crowd reaction. . . . The moment they found out the main character was gay and holding the secret back, they erupted. At first it was an audible gasp. It was followed by people screaming and cheering. It was a really amazing experience. People on the team started crying at that moment because it just felt so unreal that the storyline resonated with people so much." The performance became a catalyst for a broader conversation in the Bollywood and Indian American community and press about LGBTQ issues. In this case, and in others that have surfaced in our studies, young people are making connections among charity, civic, and political action in varied and often unexpected ways, from dedicated and sustained activities to more opportunistic and personal actions that seize a particular moment to take a stand or mobilize.

Economic and Career Opportunity

In addition to connections to academic and civic spheres, online affinity networks can also support the development of economic and career-related opportunities and networks. These outcomes vary widely—from young people finding jobs in a related industry to looser connections that involve parlaying skills and interests developed online in pursuing a career pathway. The nature of the connections varies depending on the interest area, the skills developed, and how connected the industry and marketplace are to online communities and networks. Most of the connections to careers we observed were somewhat indirect, such as when a fanfiction writer might use her writing skills in school and eventually in a career. In the case of technical specialties, and the gaming industry in particular, we see direct overlap between professional and fan networks, and gaming companies hire from their player and fan base. Finally, some online affinity networks, such as Ravelry or those that include online video, have a direct path to economic opportunity, because members can sell or monetize their work online. We take up each of these three categories of connection in turn in this section.

Not surprisingly, younger interviewees' career goals were often hazy, and they rarely articulated a clear relationship between their current activities and their career aspirations. Even so, some teens described how the activities in their online affinity networks have inspired them to consider related career paths. Like other teen writers in the studies on WWE (see the end of chapter 1) and One Direction (see the end of chapter 2), 13-year-old Abigail notes how her online fanfiction writing pushed her to consider writing as a career. "Wattpad [writing] encouraged me to expand on my talents. I would actually like to be a writer now!" Kohmata, a 19-year-old WWE fan, ruminates on various career possibilities that stem from his fan and online interests. "I'd love to be one of those internet reviewers like in the vein of the Nostalgia Critic or Spoony. I'd love to do some acting, maybe some singing too. I'd love to move to Japan and write some manga and hopefully eventually play a role in anime adaption."

Some older teens and young adults in our study chose college majors and career pathways that grew out of their online affinity networks. For example, AMV editor XStylus, a 28-year-old white male, went to college in hopes of entering the JET program, which sends college students to Japan to teach English. He decided to major in film and video because of his interest in AMVs and has gone on to pursue a career in digital video (see the end of chapter 3 for the case study). The case of Maria, who was a fantasy wrestling writer (see the end of chapter 1), is also a case in point. Once she gained an interest and skill in writing through her online affinity networks, she confided to her teacher, who suggested she write for the school newspaper. Eventually she decided to pursue a college degree in which she could specialize in technical writing. Although the social networks and cultural capital of fan writing and technical writing have little overlap, Maria was able to make this connection because of the bridging and brokering role that educators and formal education played in her life.

We saw a similar dynamic with now 19-year-old Adrian, a white male from California, who was active with *Nerdfighters* both online and in his local community (see the case study at the end of this chapter). His interest in online video propelled him to enroll in a film department at college, where he found a professor who was interested in new media. He built a web video resource library, and he describes this project as "a way for me to formalize and promote my ongoing personal study of web video." He now has an independent YouTube channel to which he uploads several videos a month. Adrian participated in several web video conferences, is writing an independent academic article, and is working on a syllabus on new media literacy, both for the university level and for middle school. He hopes to transfer to a university with a division that specializes in new media, where he can continue to write and make videos, and to minor in education so he can teach new media literacy in classrooms or write for an educational web series. Like Maria, Adrian parlayed the skills developed in his online affinity network into a career pathway, with the help of supportive educators and college programs.

We also saw examples of technical skills and social connections from online affinity networks connecting directly to professional lives and vice versa. Several AMV editors Ito interviewed had media and technology-related jobs that were complementary to their AMV interests. *Nerdfighter* Adrian secured an internship at a video-editing studio after the executive producer of the company saw his video work. This crossover is most prominent in the gaming cases, because the professional game industry and player networks are highly connected. The developers we interviewed at Blizzard and Media Molecule for the *Star-Craft II* (chapter 1) and *LBP2* (chapter 3) studies both noted that their companies hire from player and modding communities. A favorite example at Media Molecule is its hiring of an 18-year-old construction worker in England who was creating sophisticated levels in the game and sharing them online. A developer notes, "It's like a kid playing basketball in the streets someplace and thinking he could grow up and be in the NBA. They make you feel kind of that way, I think." Another developer we interviewed, Andy Bond,[4] was able to secure an internship at Blizzard after the modding tools he created for *Warcraft 2* and *StarCraft II* garnered attention and acclaim. After he interned for two summers as a college student, Blizzard offered him a job. He "decided to accept, because [he] felt like [he] was learning more on the job and on [his] own than [he] was where [he] was going to school." One of the contributors to this book, Tim Young, also developed a career pathway in the gaming industry after being an active participant in the *StarCraft II* online affinity network. Through the network of contacts he developed in his gaming community, he was able to eventually secure a job at the game-streaming company Twitch, which integrated his research training with his gaming interests and background. Unlike the examples of Maria and Adrian, the connections to gaming industry opportunities did not require the bridging and brokering functions of educational organizations, because industry and player networks are already highly connected and share a similar culture and values.

A final category of connection is linked to new opportunities for entrepreneurism tied to the growth of online publishing and ecommerce. Increasingly, online platforms and communities offer opportunities to sell items and earn income online in a way that is integrated with the online affinity network (see figure 4.2). This integration was most apparent in the case of Ravelry (see the *Hogwarts at Ravelry* case study at the end of this chapter). Briana,[5] a 25-year-old white Raveler from Utah, was able to capitalize on her interest in knitting and crochet. She started by selling booties and headbands on Etsy, an ecommerce site for handmade and vintage items. Shortly after learning to crochet, however, she found that pattern selling was a more lucrative source of income than selling finished items such as booties. The time invested in making and selling booties typically results in earning less than minimum wage. For patterns, though, once a pattern is written and published, its designer can sell an infinite number of copies. Briana investigated running an Etsy shop and found one similar to what she had in mind. She looked at the number of sales from that shop, which totaled $7,450 in less than

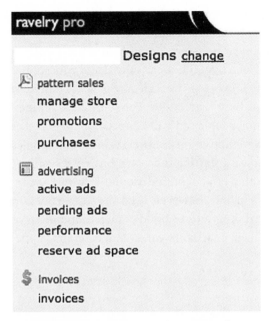

Figure 4.2. *Ravelry* makes it easy for pattern sellers to reserve their own ad space.

Image from Ravelry.com.

one year, and estimated that the shop owners made more than $80,000 from pattern sales. This motivated her to turn away from selling finished items and to begin designing and selling patterns. When Briana was interviewed a year later, she was making more than $1,600 a month in pattern sales.

Amy, a 17-year-old white teen from Colorado, featured in chapter 1, is another example of a young Raveler selling patterns online. She is only beginning to sell patterns but hopes to build an audience through a knitting blog. Sean "Day[9]" Plott, a white 25-year-old from California, also embodies this entrepreneurial spirit (see the *StarCraft II* case study at the end of chapter 1). He turned his daily webcast for *StarCraft* into a business through which he runs a popular site dedicated to commentaries and screencasts analyzing *StarCraft II* strategies. Now Sean is a successful professional screencaster and web celebrity.

Our examples of young people tying their interests to career and economic opportunity are diverse but share some important underlying patterns. In all cases, young people needed concrete forms of organizational connections and relationships to build these pathways. Many young people may have a hazy desire to become a writer, artist, or coder, but only those who have the social capital and educational opportunities that can broker and bridge to such career opportunities are able to successfully pursue these aspirations. For some communities, such as those in gaming, young people can build directly on the social capital that they develop in their online affinity networks. More entrepreneurial youth can take the leap toward starting their own businesses online if their affinity networks have that kind of online economic infrastructure. The vast majority of young people, however, need the support of family, educators, and educational programs to build connections and develop a pathway that connects their interests to career and economic opportunities.

Conclusion

Building on the analysis in the prior chapters of how online affinity networks function, this chapter has focused on how these practices and interests can connect to social networks, skills, and valued practices outside of the online affinity network. We see tremendous value inherent in the online affinity networks themselves and in the relationships, skills, and knowledge young people develop there. We all thrive by having spaces where we connect with others around shared passions and for noninstrumental purposes, and much of the pleasure of online affinity networks rests on how they are one step removed from drudgery associated with school and work. At the same time, we see promise in the largely untapped potential in how online affinity networks can fuel learning that helps young people find their place in the wider world: through academic achievement, contributions to civic and social causes, and in developing a career and economic capital. This chapter has puzzled over the dynamics of how these connections are built, and how we might encourage more of this connection building.

In this, our concerns parallel a broader set of concerns in the learning sciences that center on how skills and knowledge can "transfer" or be made consequential across different settings. This question of connecting learning across settings is central to the connected learning model. A growing body of research demonstrates that when young people are able to connect their interests to opportunities for civic, academic, and career achievement, the effects can be transformative. Our observations of online affinity networks support these conclusions. While the vast majority of young people are not able to fully integrate their interests with opportunities in the wider world, those who do have gone a long way toward finding their place in the world as adults. Our work suggests that as parents, educators, and learners ourselves, more intentional work to build and broker these connections would be effort well spent. How we might do this is the focus of the next chapter.

Hogwarts at Ravelry

Rachel Cody Pfister

Welcome to the magical school of *Hogwarts at Ravelry*![1] Here you will find many aspiring witches and wizards using wands, role-play, and knitting needles to craft a magical world based on the *Harry Potter* universe. You won't need a magical train or even a flying broom to access this magical castle, though. A simple casting of the "internet" spell will teleport you to this school. After you arrive, prepare to be sorted into a house, attend a welcome feast in the Great Hall, and get ready to craft!

The *Hogwarts at Ravelry* castle is bustling with activity, and ways to participate in the group are numerous and conveniently located on the group's discussion board. You can chat with fellow students in their house dormitories—named after the houses in *Harry Potter*, of course—or in the common area of the Great Hall. Mostly, though, you will find students attending classes. These are the same classes that Harry Potter attended during his time at Hogwarts, but students at *Hogwarts at Ravelry* complete their assignments a bit differently. They not only research and write about magical topics, but also use fiber crafting skills to produce something related to those topics (see figure C.4.1)! Between classes, you can find students playing the magical sport of Quidditch (with a crocheted beater stick, of course!), lounging by the lake, or even spinning yarn as decorations for the Yule Ball. You don't know how to knit a dragon, spin yarn, or use the bobble-stitch to represent that useful little gillyweed plant? Fret not; just ask your fellow students! They are always willing to help each other learn new crafts or techniques. One professor even leads a beginner yarn-spinning class in a corner of the castle, and another has useful video tutorials on her blog. So don your robes, untangle that yarn, and let's get started!

Hogwarts at Ravelry is an affinity network centered on the shared interests of *Harry Potter* and fiber crafting. The *Harry Potter* series is a popular young adult book and movie series about a boy wizard who

Figure C.4.1. Crocheted *Harry Potter* characters.
Image courtesy of Jen2291.

attends the magical school of Hogwarts. While aimed at young adults, the series' story line, characters, and morals resonate with all ages. The rich fantasy world of the series—including supplemental works and websites from the author—entices readers to envision and explore the details of the characters, school, classes, sports, and shops. The series garners a passionate fandom, through which fans write fanfiction, role-play in the magical world, advocate for real-world causes, and create or remix media related to *Harry Potter*.

Equally important to *Hogwarts at Ravelry* is fiber crafting, including knitting, crocheting, weaving, and spinning yarn. Fiber crafts date back thousands of years as a form of material production and social opportunity, such as knitting circles, and have recently experienced a surge in popularity. This popularity is attributed partly to the do-it-yourself movement and the ease of access to resources and communities that online tools and digital tools have provided.

Hogwarts at Ravelry was founded in 2009 by a 10-year-old girl as a space to combine the interests of *Harry Potter* and fiber crafting. *Hogwarts at Ravelry* is one of more than 30,000 groups on Ravelry.com, which describes itself as "a community site, an organizational tool, and a yarn & pattern database for knitters and crocheters." Ravelry.com was founded, in part, as an online social hub for fiber crafters and offers its users forums and member-created groups through which they can share their fiber crafting and other interests. Like all Ravelry.com groups, *Hogwarts at Ravelry* is built on a message board platform, through which topics are split into conversation "threads." The group is international and multigenerational. Members range in age from 11 years old to their mid-70s. Members come from all over the world, although most live in the United States, Canada, Europe, and Australia. When I began fieldwork in 2011, there were more than 850 members of *Hogwarts at Ravelry*, and by 2013, at the time my fieldwork concluded, there were more than 1,300 members. All active members were female, although there were a few active men in the group before 2011. The group comprises members with varying levels of experience, from novice crafters and those just starting to read the *Harry Potter* books to advanced crafters, pattern designers, and *Harry Potter* aficionados.

The shared purpose of *Hogwarts at Ravelry* is providing members a *Harry Potter*–based fantasy world through which they can pursue their *Harry Potter* and fiber crafting interests. The affinity network uses role-play, narrative, crafting, and elements of the *Harry Potter* series to build a fantasy world that parallels the magical school Hogwarts. Members role-play as students, teachers, or staff of this school and are sorted into the four houses of the *Harry Potter* series. The main practices of the group are competitions and challenges. The overarching competition of the group is that of the House Cup, an end-of-the-year award given to the house with the most points. Members earn points for their houses through *Harry Potter*–based classes and challenges. In these practices, members are asked to research an element related to *Harry Potter*, craft an item representing the topic, and write a narrative tying the crafted item to what was learned. Other activities include the magical sport of Quidditch, wizarding tournaments, and role-playing games in which members fight for or against the evil Death Eater wizards. Through these practices, members delve into their *Harry Potter* interests by researching topics in the books and on fan-created websites devoted to the series. Furthermore, these competitions and challenges motivate members to further their fiber crafting skills and knowledge by offering compelling reasons to craft more, learn new techniques, and take on new crafting challenges.

Hogwarts at Ravelry members are organized into three distinct roles that are intertwined with their status in the group: leaders, staff/teachers, and students. The leaders run the group, the staff and teachers are in charge of the practices, and the students participate in the group. While the roles are relatively fluid, in that students may become teachers or staff for a class rotation and then become students again, the roles are also a marker of status, as it is the more active and most helpful of members who are generally promoted to the role of teachers or staff.

The group places high value on providing members with a friendly, fun, and supportive community in which to pursue their *Harry Potter* and fiber crafting interests. In the General Rules for the group, members are directed to provide only positive feedback and support for members' projects: "**Be nice** in general. It is not appropriate to speak poorly of anyone else's projects, nor their choice of projects. Everyone has varying levels of experience." Help and support are encouraged and are considered an important social practice in the group. More experienced and veteran members offer resources or their experience in helping out members who ask questions or run into difficulties with a project. Encouragement is pervasive in the group; when members discuss projects they are working on, other members will cheer on their progress with comments such as "You can do it!" When members submit class assignments, the teacher and other students in the class will offer verbal compliments about the work ("I love it!"), nonverbally "love" the post, or offer detailed positive compliments about the difficulty of the project or the techniques or colors used.

Members use, share, and create a variety of resources related to their interests. One member, Jen2291, a 49-year-old white woman from Arizona, created instructional blog entries and videos about crochet techniques or projects. Class teachers may link to *Harry Potter* wikis or other online resources to help students learn more about the class's topic. Members share links to knitting websites or YouTube videos to help others learn a technique. Members also routinely use and link to patterns in the Ravelry pattern database as suggestions of things to make.

As part of the group's mission to be friendly and supportive, the "be nice" rule of the group is formally enforced. The leaders and staff of the group are tasked with encouraging a social atmosphere as well as moderating posts to make sure that members are being positive, friendly, and supportive to each other. Negative comments and those that go against the "friendly and fun" atmosphere of the group are reprimanded in the discussion thread or through private messages. Members strive to create and sustain an atmosphere that is supportive of all members' crafts and levels of experience in crafting and *Harry Potter*.

Learner Story

Mary's story helps us see the powerful combination of family support and affinity networks in supporting connected learning. Mary is a white 21-year-old knitter from Canada who was exposed to fiber crafting at a young age. Her mother and her sister were both knitters, and at the age of 9 or 10, Mary asked her mother to teach her to knit and crochet. She had "liked watching [her] mom make things with yarn." After her mother taught her the basics of knitting, Mary began a knit scarf. Her interest in knitting was not very strong, however, and she felt "allergic" to crochet because she had a difficult time learning it.

At about the age of 15, Mary became interested in knitting again. About the same time, her mother found and joined Ravelry and gave Mary some yarn. That motivated Mary to join Ravelry as well. This combination of events provided a gateway into a passion for knitting and an entrance into the fiber crafting affinity network:

> My mom was on Ravelry back when you had to request an invite—I think she'd heard about it from a knitting e-mail list or Yahoo group, but I can't remember for sure. So after she'd been on for a few months, I decided to request an invite, because my mom had just given me a lot of yarn she didn't want after she'd done a clear-out of her stash—she'd tried to sell it when we'd had a yard sale, but there weren't any takers. So after a couple of weeks, I got the e-mail from the Ravelry staff with my invite, and I signed up.

On Ravelry, Mary found a community of fiber crafters with whom she could learn and pursue her knitting. She joined and eventually became a leader of Knit Teen, a knitting group for teens. She also found groups that tied her knitting to other interests, including a group dedicated to fiber crafting fans of the gaming series *Final Fantasy* and three groups dedicated to fiber crafting and *Harry Potter*, including *Hogwarts at Ravelry*.

Participating in the Ravelry groups challenged Mary to advance her knitting as she found new techniques to try or must-learn techniques for a group challenge: "I see a lot of people trying a technique or a pattern, so it gets me interested in trying it as well—like cabling. Being in the Harry Potter groups help me step out of my comfort zone, too, because the prompts for assignments can be technique-specific." Mary recounted one particular class assignment that asked her to learn about gillyweed, a magical herb in the *Harry Potter* series, and to craft an item representing it. Challenged by the class assignment, Mary used a book to teach herself the stitch but also solicited her mother's help in troubleshooting the pattern that called for the stitch. Mary's efforts at learning the stitch, despite her not completing her project, were rewarded with points from the group and a nearly finished pillowcase. "One thing I remember having to learn for a specific assignment was bobbles. The assignment was about gillyweed, and one of the options was to craft bobbles, so I started a bobbled pillow using a pattern from the book *Stitch N Bitch Nation*. I figured out the bobbles myself, but I'd asked my mom for help when I noticed that I was short a stitch in one of my rows."

When Mary was struggling with a cardigan pattern, she found troubleshooting advice from another group member. The pattern instructed Mary to construct the cardigan "in the round," meaning it was constructed as one seamless item. A group member who had experience with that pattern, however, told Mary that the cardigan should be constructed "flat," meaning the back and front should be created separately and then seamed together. This personal experience and specialized knowledge helped Mary to learn how to approach the pattern differently in the future and saved her from further frustrations.

Participating in Ravelry also pushed Mary to overcome her "allergy" to crochet. Through participating in the groups and seeing patterns in the Ravelry database, Mary found many crochet patterns that she wanted to make. Although she would initially see the patterns and think, "Argh, I can't crochet . . . but I'll add the pattern to my favourites, because I would learn crochet to make that." During our interview, Mary said, "Recently I borrowed books from the library and asked my mom for help with learning crochet—she taught me about controlling the yarn, letting the hook do the work of picking up stitches, and so forth."

By joining Ravelry and participating in group challenges, and through the support of her mother, Mary has advanced her knitting beyond basic stitches and an unfinished scarf. She has become a leader of a teen knitting group and found support for her gaming, *Harry Potter*, and fiber crafting interests. The social supports, challenges, and sharing of crafted items have supported and motivated Mary to learn new techniques, troubleshoot erroneous patterns, and even overcome her "allergy" to crochet. When interviewed, Mary said her next goals included connecting her interests to economic opportunities through designing knitware, a possibility enabled by Ravelry's allowing users to sell patterns. For now, though, Mary wants to focus on improving her craft: "But right now I still have to learn about constructing garments—especially seaming, which I'm not very practiced in."

Nerdfighters

Neta Kligler-Vilenchik

It's not easy to be a teenage nerd, even if you self-identify as one.[1] You may be interested in very different things from your peers: the Museum of Natural History rather than the mall, a band singing about Harry Potter rather than Taylor Swift, making videos on YouTube rather than watching music clips, watching two brothers on YouTube called the "VlogBrothers" chatting about world history, politics, and cute animals rather than . . . whatever it is those other kids are watching. For many of those young nerds, discovering the VlogBrothers on YouTube and becoming part of the community of *Nerdfighters*—online, and often also face to face—is like finding kindred souls in a sea of strangers (see figure C.4.2a).

One way to describe *Nerdfighters* is as an online community of young people who coalesced around the YouTube channel of the VlogBrothers, John and Hank Green (see figure C.4.2b). John Green is a best-selling author of young adult fiction, and Hank Green is a musician and entrepreneur. Both engage in a wide variety of online educational projects. Since 2007, the two brothers (inspired by video artist Ze Frank) have uploaded two to three videos a week to their YouTube vlog (video-blog) channel, about "nothing in particular," though always with their unique look and feel, including fast-paced speech, multiple jump cuts, and various inside jokes and jargon. Their topics range widely, from "How to Make Friends" to "Revolution in Egypt: A 4-Minute Introduction."

My focus in this study is the community of *Nerdfighters*—the predominantly young followers of the VlogBrothers. As the brothers' YouTube vlog became increasingly popular, the name *Nerdfighter* emerged: In one of the vlogs, John encountered an arcade game called *Aero Fighters* and mistook its name for *Nerdfighters*. The brothers' followers adopted the term to describe themselves, and since then the VlogBrothers have addressed many of their vlogs to *Nerdfighters* or *Nerdfighteria*. Through time, *Nerdfighters* came to exist as a community,

Figure C.4.2a. A meet-up of a local *Nerdfighter* group (making the *"Nerdfighter* gang sign"). Image courtesy of CalNerdCon.

Figure C.4.2b. Screen shot of the YouTube video "How to Be a Nerdfighter: A Vlogbrothers FAQ."

coalescing mostly online, on YouTube, Tumblr, or on Facebook group pages, but also face to face in meet-ups of informal local groups.

Nerdfighters connect not only as followers of the VlogBrothers but also around a broader shared identity as "nerds." They see themselves as having shared interests in "everything nerdy," varying from video production to costume design to making group excursions to the Planetarium. They share a passion around a broad universe of popular culture content, from *Doctor Who* to *Harry Potter*. Many *Nerdfighters* also consider themselves part of the wider YouTube community of video producers (see Lange 2007), where they follow the videos of other YouTubers, and many young participants create and post their own videos. Young people find their way to *Nerdfighteria* through varied channels: through John Green's books (or the popular 2014 movie adaptation of Green's *The Fault in Our Stars*), through other YouTube video bloggers, or through the brothers' multiple educational YouTube projects (such as *SciShow* or *CrashCourse*). The barriers of entry to *Nerdfighteria* are purposefully kept low. As the VlogBrothers quip: "Am I too young / old / fat / skinny / weird / cool / nerdy / handsome / tall / dead to be a Nerdfighter? No!! If you want to be a Nerdfighter, you are a Nerdfighter." At the same time, informal boundaries to participation may arise, as when participation in the *Nerdfighter* community relies on familiarity with its content world of niche popular culture or its unique jargon.

Over time, the *Nerdfighter* community has reached significant proportions—the average VlogBrother video is viewed more than 400,000 times. In the yearly "Nerdfighteria Census" of 2014, conducted by the VlogBrothers, more than 100,000 *Nerdfighters* participated. As this census shows, *Nerdfighters* are mostly high school and college age (60 percent of *Nerdfighters* are between the ages of 16 and 22) and mostly American (distributed pretty evenly across the nation, with some international presence as well). *Nerdfighters* are predominantly female—in the *Nerdfighter* census, 72 percent were female and 26 percent male. The community also has a significant number of people identifying as genderqueer, gender fluid, or questioning. In terms of race and ethnicity, the group is relatively homogenous: 85 percent identify as white, 6.5 percent as Latino, 3.5 percent as East Asian, and 1.6 percent as black.

This case study is based on a three-year investigation of *Nerdfighteria*, including 15 interviews with members, media content analysis, and online and offline ethnographic observation (Kligler-Vilenchik 2013).

"Decreasing World Suck"

As part of their shared identity, *Nerdfighters* pursue a shared social agenda, which they loosely define as "decreasing World Suck." As the VlogBrothers enigmatically define it in their YouTube video "How to Be a Nerdfighter," "World Suck is kind of exactly what World Suck sounds like. It's hard to quantify exactly, but, you know, it's like, the amount of suck in the world." This broad definition leaves much space for individual *Nerdfighters* to interpret what "World Suck" (and decreasing it) means to them. In interviews with participants, examples ranged from personal behaviors, such as being a good person or cheering up a friend, to collective acts that fit within existing definitions of civic engagement, such as donating money to charity or volunteering.

Nerdfighters create a vibrant community that builds on participants' shared interests, their shared practices, and their sense of community, and translates it toward real-world action. A prominent example is the Project for Awesome (P4A), an annual event in which *Nerdfighters* are encouraged to create videos about their favorite charity or nonprofit organization and simultaneously post them on YouTube. The first year P4A was launched, its goal was to somewhat rebelliously "take over" YouTube's front page for one day with videos of charities and nonprofits. Since then, the project has been conducted in explicit partnership with YouTube. In the 2013 P4A, *Nerdfighters* uploaded hundreds of videos, and more than 24,000 people donated money to the Foundation to Decrease World Suck—a 501(c)3 charity created by the VlogBrothers—through Indiegogo, a crowdfunding website. The donations came to $870,000, divided among the 10 causes whose videos received the most votes by the community. According to the *Nerdfighter* census (Green 2014), 25 percent of *Nerdfighters* participated in P4A, and 1.8 percent created a video for the project themselves.

P4A encourages the mode of expression preferred by many *Nerdfighters*—video production. The videos uploaded for the project vary from those by semiprofessional "YouTube celebrities" (video artists well known within the YouTube community, though not commonly outside of it), such as "The Wheezy Waiter," to those uploaded by young *Nerdfighters*, who range widely in terms of their video-production experience. One video, created by two boys in their early teens, was uploaded vertically, with their caption explaining, "I know its [*sic*] sideways but there's no way I'm shooting this again." Striving toward the inclusive ideals of a participatory culture, *Nerdfighters* promote creative production by lowering the barriers to expression and encouraging all members to see themselves as potential contributors.

P4A not only encourages *Nerdfighters* to upload videos; it also supports their creativity through structural features. On projectforawesome.com, one of the ways to pull up videos is by pressing "Random Video," ensuring that each video has an equal chance of being viewed. The website encourages viewers to comment as much as possible on the videos viewed, with more than 460,000 comments submitted to the 2013 videos. This practice stems from the early days of P4A, when "most-commented" videos would rise to the top of YouTube's browse page, but it has been kept "partly out of tradition and partly to help videos by lesser-known YouTubers become more popular in search results." "Comment-bombs" are also encouraged through the 48-hour livestream, during which the VlogBrothers and other guests feature P4A videos and comment on them with increasingly silly behavior (cross-dressing and smearing peanut butter on the face are some VlogBrother favorites). Finally, the "perks" offered to those who donate through the Indiegogo website reflect the wide range of content *Nerdfighters* are fans of, with merchandise related not only to the VlogBrothers but also to different YouTube celebrities (Wheezy Waiter, Charlie McDonnell, Meghan Tonjes), as well as art created by the wider *Nerdfighter* community.

Through P4A and other campaigns, *Nerdfighters* build on fan practices and a broad shared identity as nerds, as well as a wide but shared "universe of taste," while each individual can choose his or her own flavor or point of entry.

Nerdfighteria and Video Production

Creative production—particularly video production—occupies a central space for the *Nerdfighter* community. The creative drive can be seen as a shared trait of *Nerdfighters*; as Theo, an Asian 15-year-old from New York, claimed, "These communities are really based on creating content." Joanna, a white 25-year-old from California, described *Nerdfighters* as "a certain kind of kids" who are creative both offline and online: "They're not the kind of kids that just sit on the rug playing video games and doing nothing else, these kids are like 'I'm going to film something' or 'I'm going to write a song' or 'I'm going to do this thing' and they're all just really proactive."

Lange and Ito (2010) discuss the "trajectories of participation" underlying creative production, including stages that move from tinkering and playing to acquiring more advanced skills. *Nerdfighters* highlight the importance of the group context in helping participants move along these "trajectories." As Inez, a 16-year-old Latina *Nerdfighter* vlogger from a California border town, explained, key steps in such a trajectory include creating a YouTube channel and uploading one's own content: "I have my own channel, which I started before I got into VlogBrothers, and I never, I just got it for favoriting videos and liking stuff, commenting and stuff like that. I subscribed to a couple of people, but after I got into VlogBrothers, it's when I started making content."

Nerdfighters are embedded in the wider video-creator community of YouTubers, but they occupy a niche genre within this community; specifically, their videos are closely inspired by the VlogBrothers' own mode of creative production in terms of their structure and tone. Examples include keeping their vlogs to no longer than four minutes or using some of the VlogBrothers' recurring genres (e.g., "thoughts from places"). *Nerdfighter* YouTube channels can often be identified by their reference to common terms in their titles, such as "nerd," "awesome," and "cool." Another notable influence is the use of "collab channels," or YouTube channels that are shared by several people who each vlog on a certain day of the week.

Collab channels can be seen as helping young people overcome some of the challenges of online production (see figure C.4.2c). Creative production is a high-effort endeavor. Producing a video involves multiple stages of planning, scripting, filming, editing, posting, and tagging. Being in charge of creating one video a week is a much lower bar than trying to maintain daily content, which was the format the VlogBrothers adopted their first year of vlogging (and which many

Figure C.4.2c. "Five Unknown Nerds"—an example of a *Nerdfighter* collab channel on YouTube.

Image courtesy of Five Unknown Nerds.

YouTubers still attempt during the month of April for "VEDA"—vlog every day in April). Members of collab channels often set a theme for the week (e.g., "the Oscars" or "your first kiss") that solves the problem of deciding what to talk about. Being assigned a regular day means you have a responsibility to the other group members, and you do not want to disappoint them. Some collab channels even impose playful "punishments" for not creating a video on your day, often consisting of dare-like tasks such as smearing peanut butter on your face while talking.

In his discussion of digital media creation in schools, Peter Levine (2007:129) notes the "audience problem": Many civic education projects online reach a frustratingly limited viewership. "We communicate in a public voice in order to address someone, and it matters who listens. It is discouraging to build something if no one comes," Levine explains. Like many other YouTube video producers, some *Nerdfighters* show interest in the size of their audience as a form of status and recognition. Yet at the same time, other *Nerdfighters* have explicitly explained that they vlog *not* for the goal of reaching a high number of views, but as a mode of expression and interpersonal communication with other *Nerdfighter* friends.

Through their community, *Nerdfighters* overcome the "audience problem" in several ways. First, *Nerdfighters* serve as each other's audiences.

The common etiquette of *Nerdfighter* reciprocity states that if someone subscribes to your channel, you should subscribe to his or hers. Beyond subscribing, a level of active engagement is the cultural norm. As Joanna, the white 25-year-old from California, explains: "I think within the Nerdfighter community, you know when you have this video and you post it . . . they're going to watch it and they're going to, like, talk to you about it. If you're talking about something that they can relate to they are going to comment back and you're going to create that sort of friendship and that connection."

This engagement, moreover, is sustained by norms of encouragement and friendliness, in which, as Joanna further described, "everyone's really accepting and welcoming." Receiving positive, encouraging reactions to videos is an incentive for further production, whereas criticism, cynicism, or meanness (the behavior of "haters" in the YouTube jargon) inhibits expression. *Nerdfighters* shelter most community members from some of the harsh reactions confronting other amateur creative production on large, public sites such as YouTube.

Learner Story

Adrian, a white male from California, was first interviewed as a 17-year-old high school senior. At the time, Adrian was an active *Nerdfighter*—he participated in a local *Nerdfighter* group and attended all of its meet-ups, and he also played Quidditch (the sport from *Harry Potter*, with brooms, but without flying) on weekends with *Nerdfighter* friends. Adrian was involved in a range of creative activities: He created LEGO stop-motion animation videos, engaged in luthiery—making his own instruments (specifically ukuleles, which are quite popular in *Nerdfighteria*)—and vlogged on a collab channel.

Adrian became involved in *Nerdfighteria* through online participatory culture more broadly. He got a laptop when he was 11 years old and looked for things he liked—he found a LEGO blog and discovered that you could talk to people through the comment section. While looking for new content on YouTube, he found the VlogBrothers and thought that they were "interesting people who had intelligent things to say and fun videos to watch, that sort of get you thinking about stuff." He subscribed to the VlogBrothers' channel, and, as part of becoming a devoted *Nerdfighter*, went back and watched all the VlogBrothers videos since 2007. "I went through and watched all of them that I hadn't seen. It was over winter break and I just, that's all I did for two days . . . it felt like I had this duty that I had to fulfill." When Adrian attended his first face-to-face meet-up with *Nerdfighters*, he enjoyed seeing the online phenomenon manifested off-screen: "It's cool on the internet but there is a certain quality about seeing these people in real life." He joined a collab channel, where he was responsible for uploading videos one day a week. He enjoyed the informal vlogging he and his fellow collab channel members engaged in, but he also wanted to achieve a higher quality of videos: "You need inspiration. You need a good idea to talk about, or else it's not really interesting."

At Adrian's high school there were not a lot of *Nerdfighters*, and he thought there was a stigma against having online friends. But within *Nerdfighteria* he found people who had a common interest in online communication and making friends. Adrian thought of his online community as a little wider than *Nerdfighters* to include the broader YouTube community of video producers. "I've got friends who I'm not sure identify as Nerdfighters, but we're all sort of part of the same online community." Through his experience with video production, Adrian also secured an internship at a video-editing studio—the executive producer of the company, whose daughter went to school with Adrian, saw his video work and offered him the job. Adrian said that commercial editing would be the kind of work he'd like to eventually do—or so he thought at the time.

Two years later, I reconnected with Adrian, now 19. During this time, Adrian had connected his interest in online video and his involvement in the YouTube community to his academic and professional life—though this was at times a challenging task.

After finishing high school, Adrian enrolled in the film department at a midwestern college, where he wanted to focus on producing for the web. However, he thought that people in his department "would openly laugh at the idea. . . . There wasn't much respect for new media platforms, or really anything except the 'fine art' of film." Disappointed, Adrian left that department, and in a TV department at the same school found a professor who was working hard to introduce a new media curriculum. Under the guidance of this professor, Adrian conducted an independent study project with the aim of building an online resource library for people who want to study web video. As part of that project, he created a website hosting a "new media resource library," compiling both academic literature and multimedia resources related to the study of digital media. On the website, Adrian explains that the project is "a way for me to formalize and promote my ongoing personal study of web video." Adrian worked on this project for several months. However, when the professor Adrian had worked with left to take another job, Adrian felt he had "no support left at the school." He transferred to a new college in Southern California to "continue my independent work and be closer to the web video industry."

As he's waiting to start the school year at his new school, Adrian is working on several independent projects. He now has an independent YouTube channel where he uploads several videos a month around topics that interest him, such as "How We Talk about YouTube," "The Science and Dangers of YouTube Celebrity," and "How to Build a YouTube Community." Adrian participated in several web video conferences, for example, as a host on a "Young YouTubers" panel at VidCon. He's also working on writing an independent academic article tentatively called "Notes toward a Critical Understanding of Vlogging," and he is working on a syllabus on new media literacy, both for the university level and for middle school. He hopes to transfer schools again, to a university with a division that specializes in new media, where he can continue to write and make videos, and also to minor in education so he can teach new media literacy in classrooms or write for an educational web series.

Adrian is no longer a very active participant in *Nerdfighteria*, but he sees the experience as central to his current endeavors: "My participation in Nerdfighteria definitely sparked the flame for all the work I'm doing. Though I don't participate very much anymore, I still appreciate that Nerdfighteria is one of (if not the) most fully realized participatory cultures out there." One of the most valuable contributions that *Nerdfighteria* made to him was "being in a very diverse and accepting community," which was "a huge confidence-booster." He explains: "I feel capable to do the kind of independent work that I'm doing now thanks to the support of lots of friends to whom the work directly relates."

Adrian concludes with a vision of the future: "I've been engaged in web communities for nearly 9 years, and those communities have had a profoundly positive effect on my life. My hope is that now, at the onset of the growing phenomenon of new media, I can help set a precedent for an open, responsible community of media participants."

5

Moving Forward

Connections to Practice and Design

Tal is a sixth grader who enjoys writing and drawing and playing games, particularly *Minecraft*. She is also a student at Quest to Learn in New York City, a unique public school codesigned by educators and game designers, including one of the authors of this book, Katie Salen. Tal learned about *Minecraft* at school and quickly became attached to it because it allows her to build and be creative within a multiplayer social online environment. In *Minecraft*, players mine and craft items, use blocks to build structures, and organize a wide range of activities that are both collaborative and competitive in nature. Tal started playing *Minecraft* at her cousin's house and eventually helped start a *Minecraft* club at school. Given the school's support for games-based learning, educators embraced the club and set up a server so the students could play together and access their online world from both home and school. Unlike the other learners whose stories form the basis of the research for this book, we learned about Tal through an environment specifically designed to support connected learning, Quest to Learn.

In addition to being active in the school's *Minecraft* club and server, Tal was also part of the kinds of online affinity networks that we have studied for this book. She learned from open online resources for *Minecraft*, which include massive numbers of YouTube videos, forums, wikis, and other server communities. Based on ideas gleaned from these online resources, Tal was inspired to write scripts for her friends at school to perform and record as animated plays in *Minecraft*. One of her teachers, recognizing the creativity and learning potential of Tal's scriptwriting, encouraged her to share the work in class, and she was interviewed about it for the online school newspaper. With the support of her peers, family, and teachers, Tal continued to pursue her writing interest and began writing every day, eventually enrolling in a summer program for writers so she could continue writing during her break. For

Tal, online affinity networks were linked to a broader network of intergenerational, local, and institutional supports, resulting in powerful learning as well as expanding her educational opportunities.

Like Tal, millions of young people around the world are passionate about *Minecraft* and connect through online affinity networks, bonding with peers, engaging in creative production, collaborating, organizing, and developing school- and career-relevant skills. Some of these youth are growing up in high-tech and wealthy families who understand the learning potential of digital games and enroll them in summer *Minecraft* camps or help them advance their skills at home. Very few of them, however, attend a school like Quest to Learn, which embraces games-based learning and encourages links between recreational in-home gameplay and school achievement. Tal's story offers us a glimpse into a world where parents, educators, and our public learning institutions work more explicitly, intentionally, and actively to connect with young people's new media interests and leverage the power of learning with online affinity networks. How can parents and educators best recognize and connect with the learning in online affinity networks? What are barriers that keep us from tapping this potential, and what are ways we can address these barriers?

As part of a broader effort in researching and designing for connected learning, we have focused our investigation on the positive learning potential of online affinity networks in order to understand learning opportunities and challenges related to a changing digital landscape. Our focus was not on educational programs, policy, or parenting, but an important aim of our work has been to offer research and recommendations that can inform parents and educators who are seeking to support connected learning for all youth. We have celebrated the creativity, technical sophistication, civic engagement, and varied expertise that flourish in certain online affinity networks. At the same time, we are concerned about the lack of intergenerational connection in many of these online affinity networks, their disconnection from schools and career opportunity, and inequitable access to these learning opportunities. In this concluding chapter, we describe our design framework in relation to the findings from our case studies, and then we consider the opportunities and challenges in realizing the full potential of online affinity networks for connected learning. This chapter pivots from reporting empirical findings to explicating opportunities for action and the social change agenda of connected learning.

Learning as Connection Building

Our research underscores a central insight of connected learning and sociocultural learning theory: Transformative and resilient forms of learning are embedded in a web of social relations, meaningful projects, and shared activities with which a learner feels a sense of affinity. Unlike the majority of learning research, our cases center on youth interests rather than educational institutions or school-related subjects. Thus collective action, social connectedness, and cultural relevance are central to the learning that we have seen in the online affinity networks we examined. Placing interests and affinity at the center of the investigation offers a different perspective on long-standing concerns about interest development and learning transfer. Our cases enable us to highlight how interest development is grounded in shared cultural identity and joint activity. In turn, this perspective enables us to consider how learning transfer can be reconceptualized as a process of cultural translation and connecting social networks rather than as a process located primarily in individual cognition and competency.

Learning in the online affinity networks we studied begins with attraction to and affinity with a shared culture and identity. Some participants go on to gain a deeper understanding of subcultural practices and form relationships with people in the network, and they develop a sense of belonging, eventually sharing work online, taking on roles in a community, and developing reputation and status in the network. Shared purpose is structured around activities such as competition, creative production, and community organizing, providing a context for ongoing activity that further bonds participants. The sense of belonging and bonding can be a powerful driver of participation and learning as young people earn recognition from others who "get it" and share a similar culture and values. Learning—gaining knowledge, developing expertise, collaborating, and community organizing—is a natural byproduct of this ongoing participation. As prior work in situated learning has argued, learning is part and parcel of participation in communities of practice (Lave and Wenger 1991; Wenger 1998). Unlike professional communities of practice and formal education, however, online affinity networks are "intentional" communities that center on shared interest, affinity, and collective action, rather than being driven by primarily instrumental or achievement-oriented goals.

It is tempting to describe this learning and interest development as a pathway or pipeline. When we put interests and affinity at the center of the investigation, however, we see how journeys through interests, peer engagements, and achievement are meandering and undetermined. A young person might discover a new interest through a school-sponsored structured activity, a parent or a peer, or a serendipitous discovery in an online search or stroll through an urban environment. That young person might abandon an interest for quite some time, only to reactivate it when an opportunity arises to make a contribution to a family or a school project, or if he or she connects with a new friend who shares that interest. As we searched for "pathways," "transitions," and "trajectories," we found these linear narratives to be elusive. When young people are pursuing interests through voluntary activities, their pathways are divergent and unpredictable, unlike what we see in formal education. Instead, we look more at broader ecosystems that they participate in, and we rely on metaphors of affinity networks, bridging social capital, and consequential connections. We see connected learning not as a journey of individual development that is transferrable across the different settings that a person moves through, but as building stronger, more resilient, and diverse social, cultural, and institutional relationships through time.

For some young people, online affinity networks are rich sites for developing unique forms of bonding social capital, sites where they feel a strong sense of affinity and belonging but in a way that can be compartmentalized from networks in their local community. These subcultural qualities and the compartmentalized nature of the relationships mean, however, that the majority of the learning in online affinity networks is not connected to local settings and communities, and it is difficult to translate into cultural referents that are relevant for academic and career advancement. Even in our cases, which were selected for their potential for connected learning, the online social networks rarely overlap with the social networks in school or the local community, or with career networks. Building these connections requires concrete forms of sponsorship, translation, and brokering in order to connect interests to opportunity. We saw examples of young people connecting their interests to opportunity by deploying the writing, mathematical, creative, communication, and problem-solving skills developed in their online affinity networks to school, civic, or career-relevant settings, and vice versa. In other cases, they were able to directly connect their interests to opportunity by monetizing their creative work or finding a job in their interest area. Sometimes a parent, educator, or mentor helped broker these connections. While we saw great promise in these examples of young people being able to connect and bridge from interests to opportunity, they were rare.

This kind of productive network building requires the agency and interest of the learner, as well as the collective efforts of those of us invested in developing learning environments and opportunities. When we consider the resources and supports that young people need to connect their interests to opportunity, equity becomes of critical concern. Wealthy parents spend increasing amounts of money on supporting out-of-school learning tailored to personal interest (Duncan and Murnane 2011), and studies indicate that these children of higher-income families are much more likely to report having a wide range of informal adult mentors (Bruce and Bridgeland 2014). Research on family investments in enrichment activities indicates gaps and differences based on socioeconomic and other factors. Lareau's fieldwork in the 1980s describes differences between middle-class families and lower-income families in the emphasis they place on enrichment and "concerted cultivation" (2003). More recent research, however, indicates that lower-income families also place a high value on athletics, arts, and other forms of enriched and specialized learning, though they may not have the resources or time to support these activities in ways that more privileged families do (Bennett, Lutz, and Jayaram 2012). While we may debate whether these differences are driven purely by economics or by values and preference, research is consistent in pointing to a gap in the relative investments of wealthy and poor families in structured enrichment activities (Weininger, Lareau, and Conley 2015).

Although some young people are able to advocate for and translate their interests into opportunity in school and career, most need the support of local programs, mentors, and parents with the relevant social capital to broker these connections. If this process continues to play out as a private, market-driven process, the growth of informal online learning will exacerbate the equity gap, reducing the odds that lower-income youth will be able to pursue higher education and career opportunities in areas that they are genuinely interested in and passionate about. The responsibility of providing mentorship, brokering, and connection building to link youth interests to opportunity is a collective one and cannot be shouldered only by families, nor only by schools and other public educational institutions. It entails a broader cultural shift toward recognizing the new learning dynamics of a networked era, paying more attention to learning and equity in online communities and platforms, and providing more educational supports in both informal and formal learning environments. Here we can only scratch the surface of the complex, systemic change that is needed for a more equitable distribution of networked learning opportunity. In the remainder of this chapter, we describe some of the significant barriers that need to be addressed to realize fuller and more equitable access to the learning opportunities of online affinity networks, and then we describe some ways and design principles for addressing these challenges.

Risks and Challenges

We have described the features of online affinity networks that support connected learning as interest-driven, socially connected, and meaningful. This book has highlighted the compelling learning dynamics and features of the environments we examined, and how they differ from more traditional learning settings. While recognizing these positive features and their potential, understanding the barriers and challenges that accompany young people's growing participation in online networks is also critically important. Many concerned with the rise of online communication have pointed out problems, such as loss of traditional reading and writing skills (Bauerlein 2008; Carr 2010), risky online behavior (Sales 2016), social isolation (Turkle 2011), or young people falling in with the wrong crowd online (Steyer 2012). We fully recognize that there are risky and undesirable ways that young people can interact online, but we have chosen a focus of investigation that points toward solutions and engagement with youth culture. Unless complemented with positive alternatives, relentless critique and denigration of youth online life can create a divisive climate between adults and young people. Too often, digital culture and devices act as a wedge issue between generations. We seek to underscore the tremendous diversity in how young people are engaging online and the importance of highlighting and fostering learning dynamics that are often invisible or poorly understood by prior generations.

Our concerns center on the unrealized potential of connected learning with online affinity networks. We see young people from all walks of life highly engaged with interests, with strong motivations to learn and to communicate and connect with others with shared interests and concerns. Yet only a small minority of young people, those who generally have high degrees of family or local support for their interests, are connecting their engagements with online affinity networks to recognition and opportunity outside of the affinity network. If this is the case with the selective sample of positive online-learning settings that we sought out, it means that the potential for this kind of connected learning is largely unrealized. Of particular concern is how, just as with early forms of digital opportunity, more economically and educationally privileged youth are taking fuller advantage of the learning opportunities afforded by online affinity networks.

Inequitable access to progressive learning opportunity is not new, but digital networks have the potential to radically expand the equity gap. When we celebrate pint-sized YouTube celebrities and digital activists, tween coding savants, or youth who are many grade levels above their peers in math thanks to open learning platforms such as Khan Academy, we should pause to consider whether these opportunities for accelerated learning and recognition are accessible to all youth. Tech-savvy and "creative class" families have been the first to embrace an ethos of digital learning that values digital tinkering and geeking out online, and parents in these families are often well connected with their children's digital interests. The internet gives superpowers to those youth who are either highly motivated and interest-driven or have a home and school environment that fosters and supports these forms of personalized, empowered, and specialized learning. This emerging dynamic is particularly distressing because today's online networks offer learning supports that are freely accessible and cater to a diverse range of interests and identities. In theory, this means that young people from diverse backgrounds and with less economic privilege should be able to capitalize on these opportunities. Unfortunately, existing forms of privilege and stratification structure access in powerful ways, even in the absence of economic and technical barriers (Reich and Ito 2017).

These long-standing forms of stratification are further complicated by the fact that online affinity networks are not commonly recognized as potential sites of learning opportunity, creating challenges in building intergenerational linkages and connections to opportunity. To tap the learning potential of online affinity networks, educators, parents, and technology and policy makers need to proactively engage with these forms of informal and interest-driven online learning. We are still a long way from having a shared understanding and public agenda for how the adult world can harness online affinity networks for educational opportunity and equity. We see two significant barriers that must be addressed: the digital culture generation gap and the lack of connection between online affinity networks and young people's local communities. We describe these two barriers before turning to a discussion of how we can support learning environments that address these barriers and expand access to connected learning.

The Digital Culture Generation Gap

As we documented in our earlier work (Ito et al. 2010), many parents and teachers view young people's online communication with concern and even alarm. Even in our selective sample of online affinity networks, young people seldom described parents and educators as actively supporting their online activities. The familiar tendency for young people to rebel against older cultural forms and develop youth-centered subcultures intersects with new digital technology in ways that expand the cultural generation gap. This gap is particularly evident with digital gaming, as nongamers struggle to understand and appreciate young people's high levels of engagement, often portraying the games as addictive and antisocial. We also see a wide gap with fan-related activity around contemporary media and music, though it was less pronounced with more long-standing interest areas such as knitting or WWE. Gamers and fanfiction writers described how they hid their online activities from their parents, and they would not think to share with teachers and other adults. Even in the cases of parents who supported a gaming or fannish interest, it was rare to see shared engagement across the generational divide. Contrast this to, for example, athletic interests or more traditional arts, which are a site of intergenerational connection and a place for parents to celebrate the achievements of their children. If we are going to tap the power of online affinity networks and digital interests for learning, then we need to address the digital culture generation gap head-on.

We see two dimensions to this challenge. One is a genuine lack of understanding and visibility around what digital youth culture is about. For example, a parent or teacher who has not grown up playing complex digital games such as *StarCraft*, *Minecraft*, or *LittleBigPlanet* will be hard pressed to understand what is happening on-screen, much less support or guide a child's learning in these areas. The second dimension of this challenge is one of cultural values and negative stereotypes. The negative assumptions that many attach to certain forms of digital culture are deep and challenging, particularly with digital cultural forms that are highly specialized or technically focused. Gamers and fans geeking out about specialized cultural referents and technical expertise can put off those who are not immersed in the subculture. Henry Jenkins wrote about the stigma attached to popular fan cultures well before the advent of the internet (Jenkins 1992). While more accepting of literary fandoms such as that for *Harry Potter*, the older generation tends to have a particularly negative view of digital gaming (e.g., "addiction") and girl-centered cultures such as the One Direction boyband fandom (e.g., "frivolous"). These negative assumptions create disconnects between adults and youth interests and result in a lack of positive adult mentorship in relation to these interests.

Compartmentalized Social Networks

Young people who invested time in and attention to the online affinity networks we examined forged deep and specialized bonds with peers and mentors with shared interests and developed subcultural social and cultural capital. The subcultural and online nature of these relationships and cultural referents means, however, that they tend to be specialized, compartmentalized, and different from the layered and multifaceted relationships that we develop in local community activities such as religious organizations, sports leagues, and schools. Further, because online affinity networks are far-flung and rarely have ties to formal organizations, there is little direct connection to opportunities and relationships in schools, workplaces, and civic institutions. When combined with the lack of visibility and appreciation of digital culture, this compartmentalization means that it is rare for parents, educators, and learning institutions to connect with the learning that is happening online. In other words, online affinity networks can support bonding social capital, but they have few avenues for bridging social capital between online relationships and local ones, limiting connections to academic, career, and civic opportunity.

For the cases we examined, these missed connections are a lost opportunity for linking the positive learning in online affinity networks to civic, career, and academic achievement. For online affinity networks with less positive valences, the disconnects could mean that young people are forming deep bonds of affiliation that create rifts with school, family, and community. In the most extreme cases, this means that young people could form deep bonds with others who reinforce negative behaviors and extremism. Again, we can contrast this to more long-standing and intergenerational interest areas and extracurriculars such as sports, performance, and the arts, which are appreciated by teachers and parents and will make their way onto a college application and a résumé. Further, the individuals and organizations that support these historic interests are well connected to schools and the life of local communities, increasing the likelihood of connections being brokered.

In our study, gaming culture and social networks emerged as examples of the growing connection between some online and professional networks. Unlike more traditional industries, gaming has relied heavily on the informal mentorship, peer learning, and professionalization that happen through player communities and digital networks. It has become normative for developers, screencasters, and other professionals in the industry to rise through the ranks of online affinity networks into professional jobs in the industry. We also see this phenomenon in other fast-paced digital specialties such as open-source software and cybersecurity. Further, platforms such as Ravelry, Etsy, and YouTube enable digital creators to directly monetize their creative work online.

In the absence of these direct social and economic connections, however, young people still need ways to connect the skills they are cultivating in their informal and interest-driven networks to social networks that open up opportunity for them. We turn now to some examples of how parents, educators, and technology and policy makers are actively engaging with ways to address barriers and support connection building among online affinity networks, learning, and opportunity.

Opportunities and Design Principles

We have described how online affinity networks can support shared culture, practices, and civic and creative engagements that are rich sites for interest-driven and peer-supported learning. While the interest areas and practices we described are diverse, the online affinity networks we examined share a set of common features that support connected learning: They all have a shared purpose, are project-centered, and are openly networked. By highlighting these common features, we hope to inform efforts by educators, online community managers, and designers to foster positive learning dynamics and expand access to connected learning. Here we describe the core design principles for connected learning in relation to our findings, and we offer some examples of educator-supported learning environments that incorporate these principles. We draw on these examples to complement the case studies that form the foundation of this book by introducing environments where educators have explicitly designed programs to expand access to connected learning and to connect affinity networks to opportunity in education, civics, and careers. To illustrate these shared underlying design principles, we focus on three learning environments that the authors have participated in as researchers or designers: the Scratch online community, Connected Camps, and the YOUmedia Learning Labs.

Shared Culture and Purpose

At the center of connected learning environments are a common culture and purpose that drive participation. People are drawn to online affinity networks because of shared interests and identities, and they stay because they develop a sense of belonging and shared purpose. If they choose to become contributors, they take on different roles, develop status, and earn recognition from their peers. Affinity networks that foster shared culture, purpose, and learning allow for diverse forms of contribution and participation, and they have community-driven ways of recognizing status and quality of work. Participants in these environments know who the newbies and experts are, and who is specialized in particular areas. They also have ways of showcasing and celebrating a range of positive contributions to the community. In other words, there is a shared understanding of how social and cultural capital operates in the interest area. Online affinity networks of the friendly variety that are successful in recruiting new participants also have practices and roles that center on welcoming new members and maintaining an inclusive ethos (Rafalow 2014).

These principles are evident in educator-designed online affinity networks as well as in the more youth-driven ones that we observed. For example, the Scratch online community, hosted by the Lifelong Kindergarten group at the MIT Media Lab, is designed to encourage coding, creative production, and positive learning dynamics. It has a clearly defined set of community values and actively moderates the site to maintain these values (Lombana-Bermudez 2017). The Scratch team has been intentional in how it has designed its reputational mechanics, encouraging positive commenting and enabling participants to "favorite" and "love" projects as well as remix other people's projects. The team also features projects on the homepage, and along with remixing each other's work, it enables participants to curate work into galleries and develop subcommunities. Together these varied activities and features have cultivated a growing community of computational creators in diverse interest areas (e.g., Aragon et al. 2009; Brennan et al. 2011; Kafai et al. 2012; Roque, Kafai, and Fields 2012).

Ito and Salen have been part of the development of Connected Camps, an online *Minecraft* community that fosters digital citizenship as well as specific STEM skills in disciplines such as coding and game design. The community is modeled on existing *Minecraft* server communities that center on collaborative production, but with an added layer of moderation and educator-designed activities. Connected Camps recruits teen *Minecraft* experts to be community helpers and instructors for its server and programs, and it enforces a set of community standards that ensures safety, positive digital citizenship, and inclusivity. Because it is staffed by young people who grew up as gamers immersed in the culture of *Minecraft*, the network also values the subcultural referents and status of the gamer world. It seeks to strike a balance between being a youth-driven gaming community and one that is centered on adult-guided positive values, learning, and citizenship.

We see the focus on shared culture and purpose in many educational programs that center on youth media production, service learning, arts, and athletics, but it is less evident in most formal and standardized classroom learning. In learning environments that are less interest-driven, it is more challenging to develop this sense of shared community values, culture, and purpose. The teacher and other external authorities determine content and standards, and students tend to have fewer opportunities to contribute meaningfully to defining culture and purpose. Schools commonly support this sense of shared culture and purpose more in extracurriculars and electives in which students self-select to participate. These can be organized programs such as athletics or FIRST Robotics, or more informal student-run clubs, such as an anime club or *Harry Potter Alliance* chapters of Harry Potter fans mobilizing for social good. In these examples, the school-sponsored activity is interfacing with broader affinity networks such as regional sports and robotics leagues, or fan conventions and online networks. Participants in these activities gain status and recognition in their school as well as in these broader networks. These kinds of school-sponsored extracurriculars, particularly when they are connected to broader affinity networks, are prime sites for connecting learning across settings.

The YOUmedia Learning Labs, a growing network of spaces in museums and libraries that center on youth digital media production, are also designed around sponsoring interests that connect to broader affinity networks. YOUmedia spaces embody the principles of shared culture and purpose by focusing on popular youth interests such as music, spoken word, gaming, and digital arts. They are staffed by museum and library educators, as well as by teaching artists who embody the social and cultural capital of the interest area. Much as we see with online affinity networks, young people describe the powerful sense of connection they feel with mentors who share an identity and interest, and who really "get them." The first YOUmedia Learning Lab, at the main downtown library in Chicago, serves hundreds of teens who engage in varied areas of interest with peers, mentors, and librarians. It is a drop-in space that is designed to be accessible and inclusive, but it also supports young people leveling up in their interest areas through workshops, projects, and performances. At the core of the model are a sense of shared culture and affinity and a diversity of roles and ways of participating, modeling many of the principles of online affinity networks we observed, but centered in a physical space (Larson et al. 2013; Sebring et al. 2013).

All of these efforts are addressing the digital culture generation gap by building environments where young people and adults can build shared purpose and activities centered on new media interests. By shedding light on some of the positive and underappreciated dimensions of online affinity groups, this book has also sought to destigmatize these forms of digital culture and to suggest that they can be sites for more intergenerational tolerance, if not joint engagement. This effort to connect youth interests and education is not unique, and it is part of a longer history of efforts that rely on culturally relevant approaches to addressing equity and inclusion. For example, some educators have embraced hip-hop culture for fostering literacy and political engagement (Hill 2009; Morrell and Duncan-Andrade 2002; Prier 2012). Progressive teacher networks such as the National Writing Project have long focused on engaging youth interests, and they have embraced fanfiction as a stepping-stone for developing literary skills (Bahoric and Swaggerty 2015). The movement toward bringing esports into high school and college settings is also promising, as is the growing effort among educators to bring *Minecraft* into learning settings (Dezuanni, O'Mara, and Beavis 2015; Dikkers 2015; Farber 2015; Overby and Jones 2015; Petrov 2014). In our earlier work, which involved a study of family contexts, we found that some of the most productive family engagements around digital culture happened when parents and youth were both bringing expertise to the table and when the parent was also learning, such as engaging in a shared photo or web-development project (Ito et al. 2010). A growing number of published guides offer ideas for shared tech projects to bring families together (Buechley et al. 2013; Denmead 2010; Frauenfelder 2014; Wilkinson and Petrich 2014). Projects such as Family Creative Learning, designed by Ricarose Roque and sponsored by the MIT Media Lab, bring tech-making workshops to less resourced communities for parents and children to learn together (http://family.media.mit.edu/). We hope that the stories we have shared and books such as these will help parents and educators understand, appreciate, and connect with their children around new media interests.

Project-Based and Production-Centered

Connected learning environments generally center on community-generated projects and activities. In the online affinity networks we studied, shared purpose and practices include competitions, creative production, and civic engagement. In all of these cases, participants are motivated by community impact, the value they provide to others, and recognition from others in their affinity network. In our online affinity networks, we saw knitters, writers, and game and video makers all organize competitions and contests as a way of driving creative production. Online affinity networks also organize around shared causes and campaigns. These projects and activities define community standards, and they provide an opportunity for people to develop collaborative relationships and roles in the network that are about supporting others, such as community organizer and coach. Shared projects and competitions are also contexts in which peers give one another feedback that drives improvement. Developing skills and expertise is a by-product of engaging in these shared practices and is not the primary purpose of participation. The learning benefits of participation are similar to those we have seen in educator-designed, project-based, and service learning: developing creativity, agency, and collaboration skills as well as domain-specific knowledge and competencies. More recently, the movement toward integrating makerspaces in schools, museums, and libraries has used new technology to reignite appreciation of hands-on, project-based learning.

Educators have successfully incorporated competitive and project-based dynamics in diverse subject and interest areas through math and robotics competitions, and through arts competitions such as those we saw in the Bollywood dance case. In addition to the competitive element, these challenges foster collaborative practices as participants contribute to shared projects. In Connected Camps, counselors organize design challenges and minigames in which campers hone their skills through teamwork and friendly competition. Programs in coding and design support campers in pursuing creative and technical projects that benefit the community convened on the *Minecraft* server. For example, youth can program robots in the game environment that clean up, deliver mail, and build structures. In the game-design program, counselors and campers build games as well as play each other's games, earning feedback and appreciation from the wider community.

At the YOUmedia Chicago space, creative production and performance are at the center of teen engagement. The mentors and librarians engage participants in shared projects such as developing a record label or a gaming podcast, or taking part in spoken-word competitions as a way of engaging youth in ongoing challenges. Participating in these projects provides a focus for engagement and collaboration as well as a setting where young people showcase their work and receive feedback and recognition.

Engagement in the Scratch community centers on creating and sharing creative work online, which includes games, animations, simulations, music, art, and stories. *Scratchers* interact and collaborate as part of their production through feedback and collaborative creation. Scratch is designed so that there is no direct messaging; all conversation takes place in public. The Scratch platform does not allow for collaborative accounts. However, *Scratchers* still create collaboratively using two main approaches: One approach is for the collaborators to discuss the collaboration on the publicly viewable comments and have the person who owns the project make the changes; another approach to creating a collaborative project is for one collaborator to create an initial project, and then each collaborator takes a turn creating a remix of the previous version, with other collaborators offering feedback and suggestions. Both approaches create vibrant discussion of aesthetics and technique, moments for growth and development, and implementation of a shared vision, with all activity focused on the product. In collaborative creation and individual projects, feedback is an integral part of skill development and creating social bonds. Because of Scratch's community values, feedback is given in a positive way, often describing a path forward for the *Scratcher* and the project. It is rare that a *Scratcher* receives feedback that is negative or that points out an issue without someone in the community offering suggestions for how to fix the problem. The community recognizes quality projects using the social nature of the community by giving the project "favorites" or "loves," leaving comments, remixing, or recommending it to be featured on the Explore page.

Openly Networked

An important feature of online affinity networks that support connected learning is their openly networked quality. A significant proportion of the activities of the online affinity networks are visible and accessible online, which lowers the barriers to access to specialized communities, subcultures, and expertise. Casual participants can lurk and pick up knowledge without exposing themselves. For more experienced participants, online affinity networks provide a space to connect with fellow creators and experts, publish and distribute their work, and gain a following. Communities with positive learning dynamics all have norms and mechanisms to guard against bad behavior, trolling, and the unproductive forms of criticism and feedback that often accompany open online communication.

The Scratch online community has grown to nearly 13 million registered users and more than 16 million shared projects (Scratch 2016). Aspiring creators can view the work of fellow *Scratchers* across wide-ranging interests and with varied levels of expertise. Community leaders work actively to encourage positive peer communication and collaborative design work (Aragon et al. 2009). The Scratch team has also designed a set of features that encourages remixing of projects so that *Scratchers* can build on each other's work. They are able to download the work of others, and edit and repost in ways that acknowledge the work that they are drawing from (Monroy-Hernández 2012). Connected Camps takes a similar approach in encouraging participants to build in a shared online world while at the same time enforcing positive community norms that guard against some of the risks of participation in an openly networked space. Counselors intervene in "griefing," which is when players destroy each other's creations or steal from one another.

The growth of digital interests (such as gaming, social media, and the digital media arts) and online affinity networks offers a broadened palette of possibilities for educators to interface with affinity networks. For example, the Connected Learning Alliance organized a youth art and writing challenge in collaboration with the National Writing Project, the Young Adult Library Services Association, Wattpad, and the online visual arts platform DeviantArt to encourage educators to connect their students to online affinity networks. The "Twist Fate" challenge (https://clalliance.org/twist-fate/) prompted young writers and artists to develop a story or piece of artwork that transformed a hero into a villain or vice versa and submit it on one of the online platforms. Educators and artists selected and curated finalists into a book that is being circulated through public libraries around the country. We also see a growing number of educators connecting their local programs to online affinity networks by encouraging students to post their work on YouTube, blogs, and other channels. At YOUmedia Chicago, all the programs make an effort to share creative work outside of the physical space. For example, a group interested in gaming produces a game-review podcast that it posts online. The YOUmedia fashion program ran a public showcase and documented the work on a Tumblr blog. In this way, even locally run programs can benefit from participating in openly networked spaces and connect with specialized affinity networks.

We see some emerging examples of schools recognizing online portfolios in platforms such as DeviantArt for the visual arts, or students aspiring to be video- and filmmakers seeing Vimeo and YouTube success as a stepping-stone. Some universities have taken the bold step of offering esports scholarships. As engagement with online affinity networks and digital networks becomes more commonplace and crosses generational lines, we expect that achievements and social connections from the online world will increasingly play a role in institutionalized forms of opportunity. We look forward to the day when One Direction fanfiction will make its way onto an application for college or for a job in the publishing industry. While we still have a long way to go to connect the engagement and learning in online affinity networks to the lives of diverse families and to our educational institutions, we see promising trends and inspiring efforts across a wide range of organizations and communities. We hope this book contributes to supporting and fueling the momentum of these efforts.

Acknowledgments

The research for and writing of this book were a collective effort that involved a wide network of individuals and institutions beyond those named as authors or contributors.

We first acknowledge the participation, the heart, and the openness of the members of the online affinity networks who let us into their lives during the course of our fieldwork. We hope to show the world what amazing and extraordinary things young people are doing online.

This work was part of a collaborative and interdisciplinary research network, the Connected Learning Research Network (CLRN), and has benefited immensely from the feedback of its members and advisors: Richard Arum, Dalton Conley, Kris Gutiérrez, Ben Kirshner, Sonia Livingstone, Vera Michalchik, Bill Penuel, Kylie Peppler, Nichole Pinkard, Jean Rhodes, Juliet Schor, Julian Sefton-Green, and S. Craig Watkins. Many insights embedded in this book were developed and honed during our regular network meetings. We also want to acknowledge CLRN's partner network, the Youth and Participatory Politics Research Network (Joseph Kahne, Danielle Allen, Cathy Cohen, Jennifer Earl, Elyse Eidman-Aadahl, Howard Gardner, Henry Jenkins, Lissa Soep, Ethan Zuckerman, and their talented teams), with whom we have maintained close ties throughout this process.

At the Digital Media and Learning Research Hub, housed in the Humanities Research Institute on the University of California, Irvine campus, we would like to thank the communications team (Jeff Brazil, Mimi Ko Cruz, and Jamieson Pond), Assistant Director Claudia Caro Sullivan, Anita Centeno, and Mariko Oda for their administrative support, and Executive Director David Theo Goldberg. We are also grateful for the insights of our former postdoctoral scholars, Melissa Brough and Alexander Cho, who reviewed numerous chapter drafts.

Karen Bleske, in addition to meticulous copyediting and formatting of the entire manuscript, provided invaluable help in integrating the different voices and styles of the contributors. Nat Soti clarified our thinking by rendering our ideas into beautiful images. At the NYU Press, we acknowledge the support of Eric Zinner, Monica McCormick, and countless others, as well as Julian Sefton-Green's leadership as editor of the Connected Youth and Digital Future Series. We appreciate the press's commitment to providing free and open online access to the series books and a platform for our readers to engage with our work.

This project was funded by the John D. and Catherine T. MacArthur Foundation as part of the Digital Media and Learning Initiative, and it has been enriched by the leadership and guidance of Connie Yowell, Julia M. Stasch, Jenn Humke, and Tawa Mitchell at the Foundation.

Like the subject of this book, this project was a highly networked and collaborative enterprise fueled by shared interests and affinity. During the course of five years, the Leveling Up team has gelled into a productive interdisciplinary team, and we have benefited from each other immensely both professionally and personally. Every chapter has been made stronger and more compelling by the input of each of the individual authors, and our understanding and thinking around connected learning have grown with the depth of our friendships. We were all supported by an even broader network of family, friends, and mentors who enriched our thinking and cheered us on. Your numbers are legion, and you know who you are!

Appendix

The Affinity Networks

Animemusicvideos.org

A subcommunity of English-language fans of Japanese anime create and share remixed videos.

Bollywood Dance

Bollywood dancers produce and perform in the Hindi Film Dance (HFC) competition scene on college campuses across the United States.

Hogwarts at Ravelry

An affinity group combines an interest in fiber crafting with an interest in *Harry Potter* to create a fictional universe.

Nerdfighters

A community formed around the YouTube vlog channel for brothers John and Hank Green are united by a shared identity as "nerds" and a broad common goal of "decreasing World Suck."

1D on Wattpad

Members of a fanfiction community devoted to the boyband One Direction connect through an online forum, other media outlets, and *Directioner* fan art.

Sackboy Planet

Players and game developers collaborate in *LittleBigPlanet 2* and game discussion forums to increase players' skills in level design.

StarCraft II

Players of the strategy game *StarCraft II* collaborate with the game's creators to stage major esports competitions and problem solve on game discussion forums.

The *Wrestling Boards*

Fan communities of professional wrestling practice fantasy wrestling through role-playing narratives.

Notes

Chapter 1. Introduction

1 The a priori coding scheme was derived from the framework and design principles developed by the Connected Learning Research Network in the report *Connected Learning: An Agenda for Research and Design* (Ito et al. 2013). Each researcher coded the data he or she collected, and emerging themes were discussed often in coding meetings attended by all research team members. Analysis was facilitated by Dedoose, the first cloud-based qualitative analysis platform that is designed with an emphasis on collaboration. Analysis of key constructs provided a pooled Cohen's Kappa of .91, indicating high inter-rater reliability. The case studies from the MAPP team, and Ito's prior research with anime fans, were not part of this more intensive research-coordination process, and that material was brought in more selectively at a later phase of the analysis to enrich the core findings established by the Leveling Up case analyses.

2 Collectively, the Leveling Up research team conducted 166 semistructured interviews and chronicled more than 1,500 hours of observation, which were catalogued in field notes. In addition, a demographic and media background survey was completed by 83 participants. Supplemental data from USC's Media, Activism, and Participatory Politics project include 15 participant interviews, 2 expert interviews, and 35 hours of observation for the *Nerdfighter* case study; and 120 interviews with dancers and choreographers globally (40 interviews in the United States), more than 200 hours of on-site observation, and extensive in-depth media analysis for the Bollywood case study. The anime music video case study draws on 23 interviews, an online survey with 277 valid responses, and more than 300 hours of observation at conventions and online.

3 Our earlier Digital Youth Project includes chapters that focus on more typical and casual youth engagements with social media (boyd 2010; Pascoe 2010). More recent studies from the CLRN also look at populations that are less digitally connected. Sonia Livingstone and Julian Sefton-Green's *The Class* (2016) documents the experiences of a class of students in a "typical" secondary school in London, and it finds few examples of connected learning. Craig Watkins led a study on the "digital edge," focused on youth who are struggling to connect their digital interests to opportunity (Watkins et al., forthcoming).

4 Parts of this section were originally published in Renninger and Hidi 2018.

Case 1.1. The *Wrestling Boards*

1 Parts of this case study were originally published in Martin 2014.

Case 1.2. *StarCraft II*

1 Parts of this case study were originally published in Kow, Young, and Salen Tekinbaş 2014.
2 Real name used with permission.

Chapter 2. Affinity

1 Parts of this chapter were originally published in Renninger and Hidi 2018.
2 Real screen name used with permission.
3 Real name used with permission.
4 Real screen name used with permission.
5 Real name used with permission.
6 Real name used with permission.
7 Real screen name used with permission.
8 Real name used with permission.
9 Real screen name used with permission.

Case 2.1. 1D on Wattpad

1 Parts of this case study were originally published in Korobkova 2014.

Case 2.2. Bollywood Dance

1 Parts of this case study were originally published in Shresthova, Sangita. N.d. "Yuri Doolan: Telling Stories with Meaning through Dance for Social Change."
2 All the respondents interviewed were between 18 and 25; most of them identified as (South) Asian American. Age is a sensitive topic in the Bollywood dance community, as some dancers fear "aging out" of the dominantly youthful culture. As a result, some of the respondents did not share their exact age.

Chapter 3. Status

1 Real name used with permission.
2 Real screen name used with permission.
3 Real name used with permission.
4 Real screen name used with permission.
5 Real screen name used with permission.

Case 3.1. *Sackboy Planet*

1 Parts of this case study were originally published in Rafalow and Salen Tekinbaş 2014.
2 All *LBP2* images used in this book are from promotional material provided by the game developer Media Molecule, with permission via its website.

Case 3.2. Animemusicvideos.org

1 Parts of this case study were originally published in Ito, Okabe, and Tsuji 2012.
2 Real screen name used with permission.
3 Real screen name used with permission.

Chapter 4. Leveling Up

1 Real name used with permission.
2 Real screen name used with permission.
3 Real name used with permission.
4 Real name used with permission.
5 Real screen name used with permission.

Case 4.1. *Hogwarts at Ravelry*

1 Parts of this case study were originally published in Pfister 2014.

Case 4.2. *Nerdfighters*

1 Parts of this case study were originally published in Kligler-Vilenchik 2013.

References

Appadurai, Arjun, ed. 1988. *The Social Life of Things: Commodities in Cultural Perspective.* Cambridge: Cambridge University Press.

Aragon, Cecilia, Sarah Poon, Andrés Monroy-Hernández, and Diana Aragon. 2009. "A Tale of Two Online Communities: Fostering Collaboration and Creativity in Scientists and Children." Pp. 9–18 in *Proceedings of the Seventh ACM Conference on Creativity and Cognition.* New York: ACM.

Arum, Richard, Kiley Larson, and William Max Meyer. Forthcoming. *Connected Learning: A Study of Educational Technology and Progressive Pedagogy.* New York: New York University Press.

Azevedo, Flávio S. 2011. "Lines of Practice: A Practice-Centered Theory of Interest Relationships, Cognition and Instruction." *Cognition and Instruction* 29(2):147–84.

Azevedo, Flávio S. 2013. "The Tailored Practice of Hobbies and Its Implication for the Design of Interest-Driven Learning Environments." *Journal of the Learning Sciences* 22(3):462–510. Retrieved January 23, 2015 (www.tandfonline.com/doi/abs/10.1080/10508406.2012.730082).

Bahoric, Kelly, and Elizabeth Swaggerty. 2015. "Fanfiction: Exploring In- and Out-of-School Literacy Practices." *Colorado Reading Journal* 26:25–31.

Bauerlein, Mark. 2008. *The Dumbest Generation: How the Digital Age Stupefies Young Americans and Jeopardizes Our Future.* New York: Tarcher.

Baym, Nancy. 2000. *Tune In, Log On: Soaps, Fandom, and Online Community.* Thousand Oaks, CA: Sage Publications.

Beach, King. 1999. "Consequential Transitions: A Sociocultural Expedition beyond Transfer in Education." *Review of Research in Education* 24(1):101–39.

Ben-Eliyahu, Adar, Jean Rhodes, and Peter Scales. 2014. "The Interest-Driven Pursuits of 15 Year Olds: 'Sparks' and Their Association with Caring Relationships and Developmental Outcomes." *Applied Developmental Science* 18(2):76–89.

Bennett, Pamela R., Amy Lutz, and Lakshmi Jayaram. 2012. "Beyond the Schoolyard: The Contributions of Parenting Logics, Financial Resources, and Social Institutions to the Social Class Gap in Structured Activity Participation." *Sociology of Education* 85(2):131–57. Retrieved August 26, 2016 (www.scopus.com/inward/record.url?eid=2-s2.0-84858322896&partnerID=tZOtx3y1).

Black, Rebecca W. 2008. *Adolescents and Online Fan Fiction.* New York: Peter Lang.

Boellstorff, Tom. 2008. *Coming of Age in Second Life: An Anthropologist Explores the Virtually Human.* Princeton, NJ: Princeton University Press.

Boero, Natalie, and C. J. Pascoe. 2012. "Pro-Anorexia Communities and Online Inter-action: Bringing the Pro-Ana Body Online." *Body and Society* 18(2):27–57. Retrieved August 3, 2017 (http://journals.sagepub.com/doi/10.1177/1357034X12440827).

Bourdieu, Pierre. 1986. "The Forms of Capital." Pp. 241–58 in *Handbook of Theory and Research for the Sociology of Education*, edited by J. Richardson. New York: Greenwood Press. Retrieved March 9, 2016 (https://books.google.com /books?hl=en&lr=&id=tK_KhHOkurYC&oi=fnd&pg=PA81&dq=bourdieu+1986 &ots=NVDueVtSQG&sig=hDtnTD8cORSUTNiUZ_PyxcgVkVY).

boyd, danah. 2010. "Friendship." Pp. 79–116 in *Hanging Out, Messing Around, and Geeking Out: Kids Living and Learning with New Media*, by Mizuko Ito, Sonja Bau-mer, Matteo Bittanti, danah boyd, Rachel Cody, Becky Herr-Stephenson, Heather A. Horst, Patricia G. Lange, Dilan Mahendran, Katynka Z. Martínez, C. J. Pascoe, Dan Perkel, Laura Robinson, Christo Sims, and Lisa Tripp. Cambridge, MA: MIT Press.

boyd, danah. 2014. *It's Complicated: The Social Lives of Networked Teens*. New Haven, CT: Yale University Press.

Brake, Mike. 2003. *Comparative Youth Culture: The Sociology of Youth Cultures and Youth Subcultures in America, Britain, and Canada*. New York: Routledge.

Bransford, John D., and Daniel L. Schwartz. 2001. "Rethinking Transfer: A Simple Pro-posal with Multiple Implications." *Review of Research in Education* 24:61–100.

Brennan, Karen, Amanda Valverde, Joe Prempeh, Ricarose Roque, and Michelle Chung. 2011. "More Than Code: The Significance of Social Interactions in Young People's Development as Interactive Media Creators." Pp. 2147–56 in *Proceedings of EdMedia: World Conference on Educational Media and Technology 2011*, edited by T. Bastiaens and M. Ebner. Waynesville, NC: Association for the Advancement of Computing in Education (AACE).

Brown, John Seely, Allan Collins, and Paul Duguid. 1989. "Situated Cognition and the Culture of Learning." *Educational Researcher* 18(1):32–42.

Bruce, Mary, and John Bridgeland. 2014. *The Mentoring Effect: Young People's Perspec-tives on the Outcomes and Availability of Mentoring*. (January):58. Retrieved August 26, 2016 (www.mentoring.org/new-site/wp-content/uploads/2015/09/The_Mentoring _Effect_Full_Report.pdf).

Buechley, Leah, Kylie Peppler, Michael Eisenberg, and Yasmin Kafai, eds. 2013. *Textile Mes-sages: Dispatches from the World of E-Textiles and Education*. New York: Peter Lang.

Burnett, Gary, and Laurie Bonnici. 2003. "Beyond the FAQ: Explicit and Im-plicit Norms in Usenet Newsgroups." *Library and Information Science Research* 25(3):333–51. Retrieved August 3, 2017 (http://linkinghub.elsevier.com/retrieve/pii /S0740818803000331).

Bury, Rhiannon. 2005. *Cyberspaces of Their Own: Female Fandoms Online*. New York: Peter Lang.

Carfagna, Lindsey "Luka." 2014. *Beyond Learning-as-Usual: Connected Learning among Open Learners*. Irvine, CA: Digital Media and Learning Research Hub.

Carr, Nicholas. 2010. *The Shallows: What the Internet Is Doing to Our Brains*. New York: W. W. Norton.

Cherny, Lynn. 1999. *Conversation and Community: Chat in a Virtual World*. Stanford, CA: CSLI Publications. Retrieved August 3, 2017 (http://dl.acm.org/citation.cfm?id=520240).

Ching, Dixie, Rafi Santo, Chris Hoadley, and Kylie Peppler. 2015. *On-Ramps, Lane Changes, Detours and Destinations: Building Connected Learning Pathways in Hive NYC through Brokering Future Learning Opportunities*. New York: Hive Research Lab.

Clark, Lynn Schofield. 2013. *The Parent App: Understanding Families in the Digital Age*. Oxford: Oxford University Press.

Cole, Michael. 1996. *Cultural Psychology: A Once and Future Discipline*. Cambridge, MA: Belknap Press of Harvard University Press.

Coleman, Gabriella. 2014. *Hacker, Hoaxer, Whistleblower, Spy: The Many Faces of Anonymous*. London: Verso. Retrieved August 3, 2017 (https://books.google.com/books?hl=en&lr=&id=9MpNBAAAQBAJ&oi=fnd&pg=PT19&dq=The+many+faces+of+anonymous&ots=fpfvRMbcJP&sig=oe8oyx9YbFNnYHbYRMqmfxYXsSA#v=onepage&q=Themany faces of anonymous&f=false).

Coleman, James S. 1988. "Social Capital in the Creation of Human Capital." *American Journal of Sociology* 94:S94–120. Retrieved March 9, 2016 (http://www.jstor.org/stable/2780243).

Comaroff, John, and Jean Comaroff. 2009. *Ethnicity, Inc*. Chicago: University of Chicago Press.

Common Sense Media. 2015. *The Common Sense Census: Media Use by Tweens and Teens*. San Francisco: Common Sense Media.

Crowley, Kevin, Brigid Barron, Karen Knutson, and Caitlin K. Martin. 2015. "Interest and the Development of Pathways to Science." Pp. 297–314 in *Interest in Mathematics and Science Learning*, edited by K. A. Renninger, M. Nieswandt, and S. Hidi. Washington, DC: AERA.

Crowley, Kevin, and Melanie Jacobs. 2002. "Building Islands of Expertise in Everyday Family Activity." Pp. 333–56 in *Learning Conversations in Museums*, edited by G. Leinhardt, K. Crowley, and K. Knutson. Mahwah, NJ: Lawrence Erlbaum Associates.

Cuban, Larry. 2003. *Oversold and Underused: Computers in the Classroom*. Cambridge, MA: Harvard University Press.

Daniel, Ben, Richard Schwier, and Gordon McCalla. 2003. "Social Capital in Virtual Learning Communities and Distributed Communities of Practice." *Canadian Journal of Learning and Technology* 29(3). Retrieved March 9, 2016 (https://ejournals.library.ualberta.ca/index.php/cjlt/article/view/26539).

De Kosnik, Abigail. 2016. *Rogue Archives: Digital Cultural Memory and Media Fandom*. Cambridge, MA: MIT Press.

Denmead, Ken. 2010. *Geek Dad: Awesomely Geeky Projects and Activities for Dads and Kids to Share*. New York: Gotham Books.

Dewey, John. 1916. *Democracy and Education: An Introduction to the Philosophy of Education*. New York: Macmillan.

Dezuanni, Michael, Joanne O'Mara, and Catherine Beavis. 2015. "'Redstone Is Like Electricity': Children's Performative Representations in and around *Minecraft*." *E-learning and Digital Media* 12(2):147–63.

Dikkers, Seann. 2015. *TeacherCraft: How Teachers Learn to Use MineCraft in Their Classrooms*. Pittsburgh: ETC Press.

Duncan, Greg J., and Richard J. Murnane, eds. 2011. *Whither Opportunity? Rising Inequality, Schools, and Children's Life Chances*. New York: Russell Sage Foundation.

Duncombe, Stephen. 2008. *Notes from Underground: Zines and the Politics of Alternative Culture*. 2nd ed. Bloomington, IN: Microcosm Publishing.

Eckert, P. 1989. *Jocks and Burnouts: Social Categories and Identity in the High School*. New York: Teachers College Press. Retrieved March 9, 2016 (https://books.google.com/books?hl=en&lr=&id=RtTZ23okVPYC&oi=fnd&pg=PR7&dq=eckert+jocks&ots=NWQeuKGr-v&sig=ye5Hn1kXoZa2aupLl6wgh6bJyB4).

Eng, Lawrence. 2012. "Strategies of Engagement: Discovering, Defining, and Describing Otaku Culture in the United States." Pp. 85–104 in *Fandom Unbound: Otaku Culture in a Connected World*, edited by M. Ito, D. Okabe, and I. Tsuji. New Haven, CT: Yale University Press.

Engestrom, Y. 1996. "Development as Breaking Away and Opening Up: A Challenge to Vygostky and Piaget." *Swiss Journal of Psychology* 55:126–32.

Farber, Matthew. 2015. *Gamify Your Classroom: A Field Guide to Game-Based Learning*. New York: Peter Lang.

Fine, Gary Alan. 1979. "Small Groups and Culture Creation: The Idioculture of Little League Baseball Teams." *American Sociological Review* 44(5):733–45. Retrieved August 3, 2017 (www.jstor.org/stable/2094525?origin=crossref).

Frauenfelder, Mark. 2014. *Maker Dad: Lunch Box Guitars, Antigravity Jars, and 22 Other Incredibly Cool Father-Daughter DIY Projects*. New York: Houghton Mifflin Harcourt.

Freire, Paulo. [1970] 2000. *Pedagogy of the Oppressed*. New York: Bloomsbury Press.

Ganglani, Naveen. 2014. "Wattpad: Where 'Panget,' 'Gangster' Meet Harry Styles, Obama." *Rappler*. Retrieved August 12, 2014 (www.rappler.com/life-and-style/arts-and-culture/66195-wattpad-diary-panget-dating-gangster-fan-fiction).

Gee, James Paul. 2017. *Teaching, Learning, Literacy in Our High-Risk High-Tech World: A Framework for Becoming Human*. New York: Teachers College Press. Retrieved August 3, 2017 (https://books.google.com/books?id=jjbZDgAAQBAJ&printsec=frontcover&source=gbs_ge_summary_r&cad=0#v=onepage&q&f=false).

Gee, James Paul, and Elisabeth R. Hayes. 2010. *Women and Gaming: The Sims and 21st Century Learning*. New York: Palgrave Macmillan.

Geertz, Clifford. 1998. "Deep Hanging Out." *New York Review of Books*, October 22. Retrieved August 26, 2016 (http://www.nybooks.com/articles/1998/10/22/deep-hanging-out/).

Glass, Brian D., W. Todd Maddox, and Bradley C. Love. 2013. "Real-Time Strategy Game Training: Emergence of a Cognitive Flexibility Trait." *PLoS One*. Retrieved June 9, 2016 (http://journals.plos.org/plosone/article?id=10.1371/journal.pone.0070350).

González, Norma, Luis C. Moll, and Cathy Amanti, eds. 2005. *Funds of Knowledge: Theorizing Practices in Households and Classrooms.* Mahwah, NJ: Lawrence Erlbaum.

Green, Hank. 2014. "2014 Nerdfighter Census Analysis." Retrieved August 29, 2016 (www.youtube.com/watch?v=Sh5RemPWcds).

Gutiérrez, Kris D., and Barbara Rogoff. 2003. "Cultural Ways of Learning: Individual Traits or Repertoires of Practice." *Educational Researcher* 32(5):19–25.

Gutstein, Eric. 2012. "Mathematics as a Weapon in the Struggle." Pp. 23–48 in *Opening the Cage: Critique and Politics of Mathematics Education*, edited by O. Skovsmose and B. Greer. Rotterdam, The Netherlands: Sense.

Hamilton, Kirk. 2012. "Competitive Gamer's Inflammatory Comments Spark Sexual Harassment Debate [Update]." *Kotaku.* Retrieved August 4, 2017 (http://kotaku.com /5889066/competitive-gamers-inflammatory-comments-spark-sexual-harassment -debate).

Hansen, John D., and Justin Reich. 2015. "Democratizing Education? Examining Access and Usage Patterns in Massive Open Online Courses." *Science* 350(6265):1245–48. Retrieved August 26, 2016 (http://science.sciencemag.org/content/350/6265/1245.abstract).

Hebdige, Dick. 1979. *Subculture: The Meaning of Style.* New York: Routledge. Retrieved March 9, 2016 (http://onlinelibrary.wiley.com/doi/10.1111/j.1467-8705.1995. tb01063.x/abstract).

Hernandez, Brenda, and Nicole Marroquin. 2013. *HOMAGO: A Guidebook.* Chicago: Yollocalli Arts Reach.

Hill, Marc Lamont. 2009. *Beats, Rhymes, and Classroom Life: Hip-Hop Pedagogy and the Politics of Identity.* New York: Teachers College Press.

Hine, Christine. 2000. *Virtual Ethnography.* Thousand Oaks, CA: Sage Publications.

Horvat, Erin McNamara, Elliot B. Weininger, and Annette Lareau. 2003. "From Social Ties to Social Capital: Class Differences in the Relations between Schools and Parent Networks." *American Educational Research Journal* 40(2):319–51. Retrieved March 9, 2016 (http://aer.sagepub.com/content/40/2/319.short).

Hotz, Robert Lee. 2012. "When Gaming Is Good for You." *Wall Street Journal*, March 13. Retrieved April 13, 2018 (www.wsj.com/articles/SB10001424052970203458604577263273943183932).

Hull, Glynda, and Katherine Shultz. 2002. *School's Out! Bridging Out-of-School Literacies with Classroom Practice.* New York: Teachers College Press.

Hutchins, Edwin. 1994. *Cognition in the Wild.* Cambridge, MA: MIT Press.

Ito, M., Okabe, D., and Tsuji, I., eds. 2012. *Fandom Unbound: Otaku Culture in a Connected World.* New Haven, CT: Yale University Press.

Ito, Mizuko. 2009. *Engineering Play: A Cultural History of Children's Software.* Cambridge, MA: MIT Press.

Ito, Mizuko. 2012a. "'As Long as It's Not *Linkin Park Z*': Popularity, Distinction, and Status in the AMV Subculture." Pp. 275–98 in *Fandom Unbound: Otaku Culture in a Connected World*, edited by M. Ito, D. Okabe, and I. Tsuji. New Haven, CT: Yale University Press. Retrieved March 9, 2016 (https://scholar.google.com/scholar?q =ito+as+long+as+it%27s+not+linkin+park&btnG=&hl=en&as_sdt=0%2C5#0).

Ito, Mizuko. 2012b. "Contributors versus Leechers: Fansubbing Ethics and a Hybrid Public Culture." Pp. 179–204 in *Fandom Unbound: Otaku Culture in a Connected World*, edited by M. Ito, D. Okabe, and I. Tsuji. New Haven, CT: Yale University Press.

Ito, Mizuko, Sonja Baumer, Matteo Bittanti, danah boyd, Rachel Cody, Becky Herr-Stephenson, Heather A. Horst, Patricia G. Lange, Dilan Mahendran, Katynka Z. Martínez, C. J. Pascoe, Dan Perkel, Laura Robinson, Christo Sims, and Lisa Tripp. 2010. *Hanging Out, Messing Around, and Geeking Out: Kids Living and Learning with New Media*. Cambridge, MA: MIT Press.

Ito, Mizuko, Kris Gutiérrez, Sonia Livingstone, Bill Penuel, Jean Rhodes, Katie Salen, Juliet Schor, Julian Sefton-Green, and S. Craig Watkins. 2013. *Connected Learning: An Agenda for Research and Design*. Irvine, CA: Digital Media and Learning Research Hub. Retrieved August 26, 2016 (http://dmlhub.net/publications/connected -learning-agenda-research-and-design).

Ito, Mizuko, Crystle Martin, Rachel Cody Pfister, Matthew H. Rafalow, Katie Salen, and Amanda Wortman. 2018. "Online Affinity Networks as Contexts for Connected Learning." In *The Cambridge Handbook on Motivation and Learning*, edited by K.A. Renninger and S. Hidi. Cambridge: Cambridge University Press.

Ito, Mizuko, Elisabeth Soep, Neta Kligler-Vilenchik, Sangita Shresthova, Liana Gamber-Thompson, and Arely Zimmerman. 2015. "Learning Connected Civics: Narratives, Practices, Infrastructures." *Curriculum Inquiry* 45(1):10–29.

Jenkins, Henry. 1992. *Textual Poachers: Television Fans and Participatory Culture*. New York: Routledge.

Jenkins, Henry. 2008. *Convergence Culture: Where Old and New Media Collide*. New York: New York University Press.

Jenkins, Henry. 2012. "'Cultural Acupuncture': Fan Activism and the Harry Potter Alliance." *Transformative Works and Cultures* 10. Retrieved August 26, 2016 (http: //journal.transformativeworks.org/index.php/twc/article/view/305/259).

Jenkins, Henry, Ravi Purushotma, Margaret Weigel, Katie Clinton, and Alice J. Robison. 2009. *Confronting the Challenges of Participatory Culture: Media Education for the 21st Century*. Cambridge, MA: MIT Press.

Jenkins, Henry, Sangita Shresthova, Liana Gamber-Thompson, Neta Kligler-Vilenchik, and Arely M. Zimmerman. 2016. *By Any Media Necessary: The New Youth Activism*. New York: New York University Press. Retrieved August 3, 2017 (https://nyupress.org /books/9781479899982/).

Kafai, Yasmin B., Deborah A. Fields, Ricarose Roque, William Q. Burke, and Andres Monroy-Hernandez. 2012. "Collaborative Agency in Youth Online and Offline Creative Production in Scratch." *Research and Practice in Technology Enhanced Learning* 7(2):63–87.

Kahne, Joseph, Nam-Jin Lee, and Jessica T. Feezell. 2013. "The Civic and Political Significance of Online Participatory Cultures among Youth Transitioning to Adulthood." *Journal of Information Technology & Politics* 10(1):1–20.

Kendall, Lori. 2002. *Hanging Out in the Virtual Pub: Masculinities and Relationships Online*. Berkeley: University of California Press.

Khan, Salman. 2013. *The One World Schoolhouse: Education Reimagined*. London: Hodder and Stoughton.

Kligler-Vilenchik, Neta. 2013. *"Decreasing World Suck": Fan Communities, Mechanisms of Translation, and Participatory Politics*. Irvine, CA: Digital Media and Learning Research Hub.

Korobkova, Ksenia, A. 2014. *Schooling the Directioners: Connected Learning and Identity-Making in the One Direction Fandom*. Irvine, CA: Digital Media and Learning Research Hub.

Kow, Yong Ming, Timothy Young, and Katie Salen Tekinbaş. 2014. *Crafting the Metagame: Connected Learning in the Starcraft II Community*. Irvine, CA: Digital Media and Learning Research Hub. Retrieved April 13, 2018 (http://clrn.dmlhub.net/wp-content/uploads/2014/05/craftingthemetagame.pdf).

Lange, Patricia G. 2007. "Publicly Private and Privately Public: Social Networking on YouTube." *Journal of Computer Mediated Communication* 13(1):361–80.

Lange, Patricia G., and Mizuko Ito. 2010. "Creative Production." Pp. 243–57 in *Hanging Out, Messing Around, and Geeking Out: Kids Living and Learning with New Media*, by Mizuko Ito, Sonja Baumer, Matteo Bittanti, danah boyd, Rachel Cody, Becky Herr-Stephenson, Heather A. Horst, Patricia G. Lange, Dilan Mahendran, Katynka Z. Martínez, C. J. Pascoe, Dan Perkel, Laura Robinson, Christo Sims, and Lisa Tripp. Cambridge, MA: MIT Press.

Lareau, Annette. 2003. *Unequal Childhoods: Class, Race, and Family Life*. Los Angeles: University of California Press.

Larson, Kiley, Mizuko Ito, Eric Brown, Mike Hawkins, Nichole Pinkard, and Penny Sebring. 2013. *Safe Space and Shared Interests: YOUmedia Chicago as a Laboratory for Connected Learning*. Irvine, CA: Digital Media and Learning Research Hub.

Lave, Jean. 1988. *Cognition in Practice: Mind, Mathematics and Culture in Everyday Life*. Cambridge: Cambridge University Press.

Lave, Jean. 2011. *Apprenticeship in Critical Ethnographic Practice*. Chicago: University of Chicago Press.

Lave, Jean, and Etienne Wenger. 1991. *Situated Learning: Legitimate Peripheral Participation*, edited by R. Pea and J. S. Brown. New York: Cambridge University Press.

Lemke, Jay L. 1990. *Talking Science: Language, Learning, and Values*. Westport, CT: Ablex.

Lenhart, Amanda, Aaron Smith, Monica Anderson, Maeve Duggan, and Andrew Perrin. 2015. *Teens, Technology and Friendships*. Washington, DC: Pew Research Center. Retrieved August 26, 2016 (http://www.pewinternet.org/files/2015/08/Teens-and-Friendships-FINAL2.pdf).

Levine, Peter. 2007. "A Public Voice for Youth: The Audience Problem in Digital Media and Civic Education." Pp. 119–39 in *Civic Life Online: Learning How Digital Media Can Engage Youth*, edited by W. L. Bennett. Cambridge, MA: MIT Press.

Livingstone, Sonia, and Julian Sefton-Green. 2016. *The Class: Living and Learning in the Digital Age*. New York: New York University Press.

Lombana-Bermudez, Andres. 2017. "Moderation and Sense of Community in a Youth-Oriented Online Platform: Scratch's Governance Strategy for Addressing Harmful Speech." *Medium*, August 15. Retrieved August 21, 2017 (https://medium.com /berkman-klein-center/moderation-and-sense-of-community-in-a-youth-oriented-online-platform-scratchs-governance-eeac6941e9c9).

Maltese, Adam V., and Robert H. Tai. 2010. "Eyeballs in the Fridge: Sources of Early Interest in Science." *International Journal of Science Education* 32(5):669–85. Retrieved July 2, 2013 (www.tandfonline.com/doi/abs/10.1080/09500690902792385).

Martin, Crystle. 2014. *Learning the Ropes: Connected Learning in a WWE Fan Community*. Irvine, CA: Digital Media and Learning Research Hub.

Martin, Crystle. 2016. "Impact of New Forms of Learning in Interest-Driven Communities to Future Pathways for Youth." *On the Horizon* 24(3):227–34.

Martin, Crystle. Forthcoming. "Designing for STEM in Libraries Serving Underserved Communities." In *Reconceptualizing Libraries: Perspectives from the Information and Learning Sciences*, edited by V. Lee and A. Phillips. London: Routledge.

Massanari, Adrienne. 2017. "#Gamergate and the Fappening: How Reddit's Algorithm, Governance, and Culture Support Toxic Technocultures." *New Media and Society* 19(3):329–46. Retrieved August 3, 2017 (http://journals.sagepub.com/ doi/10.1177/1461444815608807).

Matsuda, Misa. 2005. "Mobile Communication and Selective Sociality." Pp. 123–42 in *Personal, Portable, Pedestrian: Mobile Phones in Japanese Life*, edited by M. Ito, D. Okabe, and M. Matsuda. Cambridge, MA: MIT Press.

McGonigal, Jane. 2011. *Reality Is Broken: Why Games Make Us Better and How They Can Change the World*. New York: Penguin Press.

McRobbie, Angela. 1994. *Postmodernism and Popular Culture*. London: Routledge.

Milner, Murray. 2013. *Freaks, Geeks, and Cool Kids*. New York: Routledge. Retrieved March 9, 2016 (https://books.google.com/books?hl=en&lr=&id=LQePAQAAQBA J&oi=fnd&pg=PP1&dq=milner+freaks&ots=D8av2zltdw&sig=4jeNIggKu4BRITjZT _fbz5BMfHg).

Monroy-Hernández, Andrés. 2012. "Designing for Remixing: Supporting an Online Community of Amateur Creators." PhD diss., Program in Media Arts and Sciences, Massachusetts Institute of Technology, Cambridge.

Moran, Seana, and Vera John-Steiner. 2004. "How Collaboration in Creative Work Impacts Identity and Motivation." Pp. 11–25 in *Collaborative Creativity: Contemporary Perspectives*, edited by D. Miell and K. Littleton. London: Free Association Books.

Morrell, Ernest, and Jeffrey M. R. Duncan-Andrade. 2002. "Promoting Academic Literacy with Urban Youth through Engaging Hip-Hop Culture." *English Journal* 91(6):88–92. Retrieved August 26, 2016 (www.ncte.org/library/NCTEFiles/Resources /Journals/EJ/0916-july02/EJ0916Promoting.pdf).

Myers, Fred. 2002. *The Empire of Things: Regimes of Value and Material Culture*. Santa Fe, NM: School of American Research Press.

Nardi, Bonnie. 2010. *My Life as a Night Elf Priest: An Anthropological Account of World of Warcraft*. Ann Arbor: University of Michigan Press.

Nasir, Na'ilah Suad, and Victoria Hand. 2008. "From the Court to the Classroom: Opportunities for Engagement, Learning, and Identity in Basketball and Classroom Mathematics." *Journal of the Learning Sciences* 17(2):143–79.

Orr, J. 1990. "Sharing Knowledge, Celebrating Identity: War Stories and Community Memory in a Service Culture." Pp. 169–89 in *Collective Remembering: Memory in Society*, edited by D. Middleton and D. Edwards. Beverly Hills, CA: Sage Publications.

Overby, Alexandra, and Brian L. Jones. 2015. "Virtual Legos: Incorporating Minecraft into the Art Education Curriculum." *Art Education* 68(1):21–27.

Papert, Seymour A. 1993. *Mindstorms: Children, Computers, and Powerful Ideas*. New York: Basic Books.

Pascale, Richard, Jerry Sternin, and Monique Sternin. 2010. *The Power of Positive Deviance: How Unlikely Innovators Solve the World's Toughest Problems*. Cambridge, MA: Harvard Business Review Press.

Pascoe, C. J. 2010. "Intimacy." Pp. 117–48 in *Hanging Out, Messing Around, and Geeking Out: Kids Living and Learning with New Media*, by Mizuko Ito, Sonja Baumer, Matteo Bittanti, danah boyd, Rachel Cody, Becky Herr-Stephenson, Heather A. Horst, Patricia G. Lange, Dilan Mahendran, Katynka Z. Martínez, C. J. Pascoe, Dan Perkel, Laura Robinson, Christo Sims, and Lisa Tripp. Cambridge, MA: MIT Press.

Pellegrino, James W., and Margaret L. Hilton. 2012. *Education for Life and Work: Developing Transferable Knowledge and Skills in the 21st Century*. Washington, DC: National Academies Press. Retrieved August 26, 2016 (www.nap.edu/catalog. php?record_id=13398).

Penuel, William R., Daniela DiGiacomo, Katie Van Horne, and Ben Kirshner. 2016. "A Social Practice Theory of Learning and Becoming across Contexts and Time." *Frontline Learning Research* 4(4):30–38.

Penuel, William, Katie Van Horne, Adam York, Rafi Santo, Dixie Ching, and Tim Podkul. 2015. *Connected Learning: From Outcomes Workshops to Survey Items*. Retrieved August 26, 2016 (https://hiveresearchlab.files.wordpress.com/2015/05 /clrn-from-workshop-to-survey-items-report-may-2015.pdf).

Petrov, Anton. 2014. "Using Minecraft in Education: A Qualitative Study on Benefits and Challenges of Game-Based Education." Master's thesis, Department of Curriculum, Teaching and Learning, University of Toronto.

Pfister, Rachel Cody. 2014. *Hats for House Elves: Connected Learning and Civic Engagement in Hogwarts at Ravelry*. Irvine, CA: Digital Media and Learning Research Hub.

Pfister, Rachel Cody. 2016. "Unraveling Hogwarts: Understanding an Affinity Group through the Lens of Activity Theory." PhD diss., Department of Communication, University of California, San Diego.

Portes, Alejandro, and Patricia Landolt. 1996. "The Downside of Social Capital." *American Prospect* 26:18–23.

Prensky, Marc. 2010. *Teaching Digital Natives: Partnering for Real Learning*. New York: Corwin.

Prier, Darius D. 2012. *Culturally Relevant Teaching: Hip-Hop Pedagogy in Urban Schools*. New York: Peter Lang.

Putnam, Robert D. 2001. *Bowling Alone: America's Declining Social Capital*. New York: Simon and Schuster. Retrieved March 9, 2016 (http://muse.jhu.edu/journals/journal_of_democracy/voo6/6.1putnam.html).

Rafalow, Matthew H. 2014. "Support the noobs: Community Design for Inclusivity." Retrieved August 12, 2016 (http://clrn.dmlhub.net/content/support-the-noobs-community-design-for-inclusivity).

Rafalow, Matthew H. 2015. "noobs, Trolls, and Idols: Boundary-Making among Digital Youth." *Sociological Studies of Children and Youth* 19:243–66.

Rafalow, Matthew H. 2016. "Disciplining Play: Education and Youth Culture in the Twenty-First Century." PhD diss., Department of Sociology, University of California, Irvine.

Rafalow, Matthew, and Katie Salen Tekinbaş. 2014. *Welcome to Sackboy Planet: Connected Learning among LittleBigPlanet 2 Players*. Irvine, CA: Digital Media and Learning Research Hub.

Rainie, Lee, and Barry Wellman. 2012. *Networked: The New Social Operating System*. Cambridge, MA: MIT Press.

Rao, V. A. K. 1995. "Dance in Indian Cinema." Pp. 299–306 in *Rasa: The Indian Performing Arts in the Last Twenty-Five Years*, edited by S. Kothari and B. Mukherjee. Calcutta: Anamika Sangam Research and Publications.

Reich, Justin, and Mizuko Ito. 2017. *From Good Intentions to Real Outcomes: Equity by Design in Learning Technologies*. Irvine, CA: Digital Media and Learning Research Hub.

Renninger, K. Ann, and Suzanne E. Hidi. 2016. *The Power of Interest for Motivation and Engagement*. New York: Routledge.

Renninger, K. Ann, and Suzanne Hidi, eds. 2018. *The Cambridge Handbook on Motivation and Learning*. Cambridge: Cambridge University Press.

Rheingold, Howard. 2000. *The Virtual Community: Homesteading on the Electronic Frontier*. Cambridge, MA: MIT Press.

Roque, Ricarose, Yasmin B. Kafai, and Deborah A. Fields. 2012. "From Tools to Communities: Designs to Support Online Creative Collaboration in Scratch." Pp. 220–23 in *Proceedings of the 11th International Conference on Interaction Design and Children*. New York: ACM.

Rose, Mike. 2014. *The Mind at Work: Valuing the Intelligence of the American Worker*. New York: Penguin Press.

Russell, Adrienne, and Nabil Echchaibi, eds. 2009. *International Blogging: Identity, Politics and Networked Publics*. New York: Peter Lang.

Salen, Katie, and Eric Zimmerman. 2004. *Rules of Play: Game Design Fundamentals*. Cambridge, MA: MIT Press.

Sales, Nancy Jo. 2016. *American Girls: Social Media and the Secret Lives of Teenagers*. New York: Knopf.

Sammond, Nicholas. 2005. "A Brief and Unnecessary Defense of Professional Wrestling." Pp. 1–22 in *Steel Chair to the Head: The Pleasure and Pain of Professional Wrestling*, edited by N. Sammond. Durham, NC: Duke University Press.

Schor, Juliet B., Connor Fitzmaurice, Lindsey B. Carfagna, Will Attwood-Charles, and Emilie Dubois Poteat. 2015. "Paradoxes of Openness and Distinction in the Sharing Economy." *Poetics* 54:66–81. Retrieved March 9, 2016 (www.sciencedirect.com /science/article/pii/S0304422X15000881).

Scientific American. 1895. "Modern Wrestling." November 9:299–300.

Scratch. 2016. "Community Statistics at a Glance." Retrieved August 15, 2016 (https: //scratch.mit.edu/statistics/).

Searle, Rosalind H. 2004. "Creativity and Innovation in Teams." Pp. 175–88 in *Collaborative Creativity: Contemporary Perspectives*, edited by D. Miell and K. Littleton. London: Free Association Books.

Sebring, Penny Bender, Eric R. Brown, Kate M. Julian, Stacy B. Ehrlich, Susan E. Sporte, Erin Bradley, and Lisa Meyer. 2013. *Teens, Digital Media, and the Chicago Public Library*. Chicago: UChicago Consortium on School Research. Retrieved August 26, 2016 (http://ccsr.uchicago.edu/publications/teens-digital-media-and-chicago-public-library).

Seelye, Katharine Q. 2014. "Breaking Out of the Library Mold, in Boston and Beyond." *New York Times*, March 7. Retrieved August 12, 2017 (www.nytimes.com/2014/03/08 /us/breaking-out-of-the-library-mold-in-boston-and-beyond.html).

Shirky, Clay. 2006. "Tiny Slice, Big Market." *Wired*, November 1. Retrieved August 26, 2016 (www.wired.com/2006/11/meganiche/).

Shresthova, Sangita. 2011. *Is It All about Hips? Around the World with Bollywood Dance*. New Delhi: Sage Publications India.

Shresthova, Sangita. N.d. "Yuri Doolan: Telling Stories with Meaning through Dance for Social Change." Retrieved June 25, 2016 (https://clalliance.org/resources /personal-story-yuri-doolan/).

Small, Mario. 2009. *Unanticipated Gains: Origins of Network Inequality in Everyday Life*. New York: Oxford University Press.

Squire, Kurt D. 2004. "Replaying History: Learning World History through Playing Civilization III." PhD diss., School of Education, Indiana University, Bloomington.

Steinkuehler, Constance. 2007. "Massively Multiplayer Online Gaming as a Constellation of Literacy Practices." *E-Learning and Digital Media* 4(3):297–318. Retrieved August 3, 2017 (http://journals.sagepub.com/doi/10.2304/elea.2007.4.3.297).

Steinkuehler, Constance. 2008. "Massively Multiplayer Online Games as an Educational Technology: An Outline for Research." *Educational Technology* 48(1):10–21. Retrieved August 3, 2017 (https://eric.ed.gov/?id=EJ792144).

Steyer, James P. 2012. *Talking Back to Facebook: The Common Sense Guide to Raising Kids in the Digital Age*. New York: Scribner.

Taylor, T. L. 2009. *Play between Worlds: Exploring Online Game Culture*. Cambridge, MA: MIT Press.

Team Liquid. 2012. "eSports Survey Results." Retrieved August 27, 2014 (www.teamliq-uid.net/forum/starcraft-2/337149-esports-survey-results).

Team Liquid. 2013a. "Math on Widow Mines—How STLife Dodged the Shots." Retrieved July 6, 2016 (www.teamliquid.net/forum/sc2-strategy/403878-math-on-widow-mines-how-stlife-dodged-the-shots).

Team Liquid. 2013b. "Metagame." *Liquipedia*. Retrieved March 8, 2014 (http://wiki.teamliquid.net/starcraft/Metagame).

Thomas, Douglas, and John Seely Brown. 2011. *A New Culture of Learning: Cultivating the Imagination for a World of Constant Change*. CreateSpace Independent Publishing Platform. Retrieved February 6, 2012 (www.amazon.com/New-Culture-Learning-Cultivating-Imagination/dp/1456458884).

Thompson, Joseph, Mark Blair, Lihan Chen, and Andrew Henrey. 2013. "Video Game Telemetry as a Critical Tool in the Study of Complex Skill Learning." *PLoS One*. Retrieved August 26, 2016 (http://journals.plos.org/plosone/article?id=10.1371/journal.pone.0075129).

Thornton, Sarah. 1996. *Club Cultures: Music, Media, and Subcultural Capital*. Middletown, CT: Wesleyan University Press. Retrieved March 9, 2016 (https://books.google.com/books?hl=en&lr=&id=u84cOSvUADUC&oi=fnd&pg=PR7&dq=thornton+club&ots=53v5ROrAGw&sig=A6cxL2jsc-ulfMraYpqxUXiiaJw).

Turkle, Sherry. 2005. *The Second Self: Computers and the Human Spirit*. Cambridge, MA: MIT Press.

Turkle, Sherry. 2011. *Alone Together: Why We Expect More from Technology and Less from Each Other*. New York: Basic Books.

Van Horne, Katie, Carrie Allen, Daniela DiGiacomo, Josie Chang-Order, and Erica Van Steenis. 2016. "Brokering In and Sustained Interest-Related Pursuits: A Longitudinal Study of Connected Learning." Retrieved August 12, 2017 (https://dml2016.dmlhub.net/wp-content/uploads/2016/02/14_vanHorne_CLRNBrokering Paper040416_submit.pdf).

Varenne, Hervé, and Ray McDermott. 1999. *Successful Failure: The School America Builds*. Boulder, CO: Westview Press.

Varnelis, Kazys, ed. 2012. *Networked Publics*. Cambridge, MA: MIT Press.

Vincent, Michael. 2014. "25 Million Users Are Now Using Writing Platform Wattpad to Discover Amazing Stories." *Vulcan Post*. Retrieved August 26, 2016 (https://vulcanpost.com/7642/25-million-users-are-now-using-writing-platform-wattpad-to-discover-amazing-stories/).

Wagner, Tony. 2012. *Creating Innovators: The Making of Young People Who Will Change the World*. New York: Scribner.

Watkins, Craig. 2009. *The Young and the Digital: What the Migration to Social Network Sites, Games, and Anytime, Anywhere Media Means for Our Future*. Boston: Beacon Press.

Watkins, Craig, Andres Lombana-Bermudez, Alexander Cho, Jacqueline Vickery, Vivian Shaw, and Lauren Weinzimmer. Forthcoming. *The Digital Edge: How Black and Latino Youth Navigate Digital Inequality*. New York: New York University Press.

Weininger, Elliot B., Annette Lareau, and Dalton Conley. 2015. "What Money Doesn't Buy: Class Resources and Children's Participation in Organized Extracurricular Activities." *Social Forces* 94(2):479–503.

Wenger, Etienne. 1998. *Communities of Practice: Learning, Meaning, and Identity.* New York: Cambridge University Press.

Wilkins, Amy. 2008. *Wannabes, Goths, and Christians: The Boundaries of Sex, Style, and Status.* Chicago: University of Chicago Press.

Wilkinson, Karen, and Mike Petrich. 2014. *The Art of Tinkering.* San Francisco: Weldon Owen.

Woolcock, Michael. 1998. "Social Capital and Economic Development: Toward a Theoretical Synthesis and Policy Framework." *Theory and Society* 27:151–208. Retrieved March 9, 2016 (www.springerlink.com/index/rj58534767m2j644.pdf).

WWE. N.d. "Company Overview." Retrieved January 11, 2014 (http://corporate.wwe.com/company/overview).

Yeshua-Katz, Daphna, and Nicole Martins. 2013. "Communicating Stigma: The Pro-Ana Paradox." *Health Communication* 28(5):499–508. Retrieved August 3, 2017 (http://www.tandfonline.com/doi/abs/10.1080/10410236.2012.699889).

Young, Timothy. 2013. "Widow Mine Math." Retrieved July 6, 2016 (http://clrn.dmlhub.net/content/widow-mine-math).

Yune, Tommy. 2011. "Anime Fans Raise Funds for Japan." Retrieved July 9, 2016 (http://ireport.cnn.com/docs/DOC-575274).

About the Authors

Mizuko Ito is Professor in Residence and the director of the Connected Learning Lab at the University of California, Irvine. She is cofounder of the nonprofit Connected Camps and former Chair of the Connected Learning Research Network.

Crystle Martin is Director of Library and Learning Resources at El Camino College.

Rachel Cody Pfister has a PhD from the Department of Communication at the University of California, San Diego.

Matthew H. Rafalow is a social scientist at YouTube, where he conducts design-facing research on digital technology adoption among youth and young adults.

Katie Salen is founding Executive Director of Institute of Play, cofounder of Connected Camps, and Professor in Informatics at UC Irvine, where she teaches in the Computer Game Science and MHCID programs.

Amanda Wortman is the Research Manager for the Connected Learning Lab and for the Connected Learning Research Network, based at the University of California, Irvine.

About the Contributors

Adam Ingram-Goble is a Software Architect at MINDBODY, Inc.

Neta Kligler-Vilenchik is Assistant Professor of Communication and Journalism at the Hebrew University of Jerusalem. She is a co-author of *By Any Media Necessary: The New Youth Activism* (NYU Press, 2016).

Ksenia Korobkova is a doctoral student at the University of California, Irvine.

Yong Ming Kow is Assistant Professor at the School of Creative Media at City University of Hong Kong.

Sangita Shresthova is the Director of Henry Jenkins's Media Activism and Participatory Politics (MAPP) project based at the Annenberg School for Communication and Journalism at the University of Southern California. She is a co-author of *By Any Media Necessary: The New Youth Activism* (NYU Press, 2016).

Timothy Young holds a Master's of Science in Information and Computer Science from the University of California, Irvine. He is an analyst at Twitch.

Index

Note: Italic page numbers indicate illustrations.